THE HANDBOOK ON ATHLETIC PERFECTION

A Training Manual for Christian Athletes

WORKBOOK EDITION

What is the Workbook Editon?

There is a regular edition of the Handbook on Athletic Perfection, so why is this workbook edition needed?

Besides being a larger format for more notes, it's designed for one-on-one discussions or small group meetings. Each chapter has special discussion breaks for *Huddle Up!* and *Go Deep* questions to make discussion easier.

The Handbook on Athletic Perfection Workbook Edition

ISBN: 978-1-938254-33-8

Cross Training Publishing
www.crosstrainingpublishing.com
(308) 293-3891

Cross Training Publishing

TABLE OF

CONTENTS

FOREWORD

During my football career at Brown University, one of my teammates, Harry Walls, led me to Christ. A few years earlier, my high school coach had given me a copy of Wes Neal's Handbook on Athletic Perfection, but it didn't really make a lot of sense to me until after that life-changing decision. Then, it became my first devotional book as a young Christian.

Wes' book never replaced the Bible for me, but it did keep driving me back to God's Word. That's when I know a book is good—when it takes you deeper into the Scriptures and draws you into a deeper relationship with the Lord.

The Handbook on Athletic Perfection gave me everything I needed to help me understand how I could apply biblical teaching and the gospel to the world of competitive sports. It was clear that this was what God wanted me to do back then, as an athlete and now as a coach.

For many years now, my good friend Gordon Thiessen and I have done our best to continue and build upon Wes' legacy within the sports ministry community. The groundbreaking principles laid out in his book are needed just as much today as they were when he first introduced them.

While Wes Neal published his book in 1974, we have never updated the content of his book until now, 2024. We are so excited to have him update his illustrations and refresh his biblical teaching 50 years later.

Too many of us as Christian coaches and athletes have compartmentalized our faith. We act like believers before and after competition, but too often we act like the world while on the field of play. But our faith in Christ is not circumstance based. Our faith in Christ and what we learn from the Scriptures should be applied to all areas of our life—even in the middle of the rough and tumble world of high stakes athletics.

Ron Brown

Nebraska Football Director of Player Development and Outreach
Co-Founder of Kingdom Sports

PREFACE

Wes' story. Wes Neal served with the Athletes In Action ministry and traveled with their weightlifting team during the 1970s when he realized he didn't know how to "do sports God's way." His wife Peggy pointed out this fact following a routine workout when she watched Wes become visibly angry. His quest to discover how to compete biblically led him to read through the entire New Testament and organize principles into 18 different categories. These 3x5 cards became the chapters for his book the Handbook on Athletic Perfection. These biblical principles became a systematic theology of competition that spread throughout the Christian sports world during the early 1970s. Wes spoke to thousands of coaches and athletes about what he had learned from the Bible. He was a frequent speaker at Fellowship of Christian Athletes, Athletes in Action, and Kanakuk Christian camps.

Gordon's story. Gordon Thiessen was a scholarship football player at the University of Nebraska during 1975 when he committed his life to Christ. Sports had been an idol his entire life. Once he realized how sports had become too important in his life, he considered quitting them. He even considered transferring to a small Christian college. That coach realized Gordon wanted to transfer because he wanted to glorify God rather than himself. He advised him to return to Nebraska, pray about his decision, and seek wise counsel. Just a week later, Gordon entered a Christian bookstore to find answers to his questions. The store manager told him that he had the perfect book, which was Wes' Handbook on Athletic Perfection. Gordon read Wes' book cover to cover and began a bible study with his teammates using the study. He later worked for Wes Neal's ministry before serving with the Fellowship of Christian Athletes for nearly three decades. Along the way, he coached high school sports for 20 years using Wes' book. He also founded Cross Training Publishing to keep the book in print and publish more resources for Christian coaches and athletes.

Ron's story. Ron Brown grew up on Martha's Vineyard. He became one of the most outstanding football and basketball players in the island's history. He is about a month younger than Gordon, so he was also competing during the mid-1970s. While Ron grew up in a religious home, it wasn't until high school that he began wondering how faith and sport intersect. His high school coach gave him a copy of Wes Neal's book because he thought Ron would be interested in reading it. Ron played football at Brown University with a teammate named Harry Walls, known for his Christian faith but not so much for his athletic ability. While he wasn't known for his speed, he did have the best pair of hands on the receiving team. However, an injury to his hand caused him to drop to the bottom of the depth chart. He was ready to quit the team when a friend who was studying Wes Neal's book with him challenged him to reconsider his decision based upon their discussions around the book. He said, "So you're telling me that you can play for the glory of God, but you can't practice for the glory of God?" Immediately, Harry knew he needed to return for one more season. In the final year with the team, he influenced Ron Brown to give his life to the Lord. Harry later became a pastor and today teaches the principles he learned from Wes Neal, to coaches and athletes at the Master's University, where he serves as the campus pastor.

Kingdom Sports Story. Ron Brown played briefly in the NFL and began his coaching career at Brown University before being hired as an assistant coach at the University of Nebraska in 1987. Shortly after moving to Lincoln, he attended a coaches clinic where he met Gordon at the FCA booth. Gordon recalls asking Ron two things. First, why do you think God has called you to Nebraska? Second, have you read the Handbook on Athletic Perfection? From that moment until today, they have partnered to preach the gospel and teach how to do sports God's way. In 2017, they founded Kingdom Sports to teach coaches and athletes how to do sports God's way. You can find books, videos, and many other training tools at their website: www.kingdomsports.online.

INTRODUCTION

What you are about to read in this handbook is a new approach to athletic competition. Yet, the principles are as old as the Bible. In this handbook, I've taken God's tried and true biblical principles and related them to today's athletes.

Many people have asked how this handbook came about. As I relate to you its story, I hope you will become as excited as I am about its possible effect on your athletic performance.

I desire Jesus Christ to become the center of your athletic life. As you learn to fellowship with Him during your training, practices, and competitions, you will also experience a deeper walk with Him in all other areas of your life.

The Puzzling Question

This handbook began a few years ago while I was traveling the country on an evangelistic weightlifting team. I wondered if God had something to say about how athletes could reach their maximum athletic potential.

I knew there were biblical principles for reaching one's maximum potential in other areas of life, such as one's family. It seemed that God's Word would also have something to say that could apply to athletes in their quest for maximum development.

A puzzling question was, "How do I lift weights the way God wants me to lift them?" I had no answer. I knew how to train to develop greater strength, but I didn't know for certain that I was doing it God's way.

A close friend and weightlifting partner on the team, Dan'l Hollis, and I used to talk about this for hours at a time. Yet, neither of us could answer the question with any certainty. The best we came up with was, "Lift weights in the power of the Holy Spirit and leave the results up to God." Our problem was we didn't know how to lift weights in the power of the Holy Spirit. At the tour's end, I began researching the Bible for an answer.

Stack of 3x5 Cards

To my excitement, truths began to leap at me off the pages of the Bible. I wrote each passage that related to this question on a 3X5 card. Before I was through, my stack of cards was over six inches high. Then, I sorted the cards into categories. Next, I began to apply these principles to my weightlifting workouts.

Amazing Results

Immediately, I noticed two results.

First, my fellowship with God continued throughout my entire lifting session. That was a new experience for me. Those training hours had always been set apart from my fellowship with God. Now, He was an integral part of my training sessions.

Second, I noticed a greater intensity in my workouts. I had greater motivation than ever before, giving me a sharper focus. And…it was consistent day after day. My greater intensity soon led to faster improvement. In fact, I was lifting heavier weights at a reduced body weight.

Put Into a Book

As I shared what I was learning with other Christian athletes, and they experienced the same two results, I compiled this "new" information into manuscript form and wrote the book *Making of an Athlete of God.* It later became *The Handbook of Athletic Perfection.*

50 Years Later

Fifty years later, this updated edition contains all the information in the original book with some added biblical principles. I have also added several stories of athletes who have applied the biblical principles.

For example, from one college basketball player:

"Riding the bench can be pretty frustrating, especially after two years. My natural tendency is to feel sorry for myself, blame the coach, and not cheer for my teammates.

"I decided my way wasn't the best, so I decided to try to do things God's way. I realized that one reason He had me on the team was to learn how to glorify Him in tough circumstances.

"I learned how Jesus could live through me even as I sat on the bench. He gave me a positive attitude, and I started encouraging my teammates. I ended up feeling good about the season."

Four Reasons

One of the questions athletes have asked is, "Why should a Christian place an emphasis on athletics?" Many gifted athletes quit sports because they can't relate Christianity to athletic competition. Well, I see four reasons for a Christian to pursue athletics if he or she has been given the talent and interest to do so.

1. A person is to remain in the same condition as he was when he became a Christian.

"Brethren, let each man remain in that condition in which he was called."
1 Corinthians 7:24

This, of course, does not mean God cannot call you into a new area of activity. It only means that you just don't drop what you're doing when you become a Christian.

If the Lord wants you in a new area of activity, He will reveal that to you. Some of His ways of revealing are His Word, the counsel of others, circumstances, and the peace of mind that only He can give.

2. The talents you have been given are from God and are designed for His purpose.

"The Lord has made everything for its [His] own purpose..."
Proverbs 16:4

You have a responsibility to invest those talents for whatever purpose God has designed them. God will reveal that to you through His Word, counsel from others, circumstances, and continual prayer.

3. An athlete has a built-in platform for sharing the good news of Jesus Christ.

In America, athletics is a prime form of entertainment for millions of people. People listen to what an athlete says, not because the athlete is an expert on the subject, but because they have a familiarity with the athlete. People have either seen the athlete in competition or have read about them. That platform of familiarity can be used to share the good news of Jesus Christ.

C.J. Stroud, quarterback for the Houston Texans football team in the National Football League, put it this way:

"Jesus laid His life on the cross for us. I believe that. This is bigger than just football. Football is my platform. Spreading the gospel of Jesus Christ is my purpose."

4. You will understand more clearly how to apply God's Word to your non-athletic world as you learn how to apply it to your athletic world.

One of the benefits of athletics is that it is a microcosm of life. Competitive athletics provides us with a mirror for our attitudes. It's interesting that frequently, the same attitudes we show in athletics are those we show in similar non-athletic activities.

For instance, picture a golfer dribbling the ball off a tee after having taken a mighty swing. He gets so upset with himself that he takes his driver and breaks it in two.

When the golfer receives a bill in the mail, he has the same temper flare-up at home. He expected the bill, but there was an added charge he didn't expect. He reacts the same as he did when things didn't go his way on the golfing tee, and he rips the bill in two.

As you apply God's Word to your athletic performance, you will understand more clearly how to apply it to other areas of your life.

What You Can Expect

This handbook is designed to help you understand how God's Word applies to your athletic performance. You won't necessarily become all-world by diligently applying the concepts in this handbook. But you will develop into the maximum athlete God has designed you to be...living out His purpose for you.

Most likely, that will be a great improvement in your performance. Of course, you can't expect the maximum results by reading this handbook and then setting it aside. It must be studied, applied, discussed, and studied some more. However, it is only a handbook. The Bible is the ultimate source of information on God's way of doing things, for the Bible is God speaking to us.

In the chapters of this handbook, you will come to grips with the word "perfect." Now, we tend to think that no one can be perfect. But, as we will explore in this handbook, you can be perfect in your athletic performance. So, with that in mind, let's go to the first chapter to learn how!

CHAPTER ONE

PERFECTION

Picture yourself as the perfect athlete. Your skills excel compared to those of other athletes. No one is even close. Physical and mental errors are as out of place in your performance as a heat wave in a winter snowstorm. You are always in peak condition.

Routine execution for you is the perfect blend of maximum strength, incredible speed, coordination, reflex action, accuracy, and timing. Your mind sends nerve impulses through your body for just the right touch in every situation. No question, you are one amazing athlete…and a model for perfection.

MAN'S PERFECTION VERSUS GOD'S PERFECTION

Sounds a bit unrealistic, doesn't it? No athlete is perfect. Imperfections are as common in athletics as sand on the seashore.

Cicero, a Roman politician living in the century before the birth of Jesus Christ, put it this way, "Nothing is harder to find than perfection." Of course, Cicero's words might just as well have been written with the athlete in mind.

Interestingly, one of the most penetrating statements of Jesus Christ to His followers seems to challenge Cicero's words. Jesus told His followers,

*"Therefore, you are to be **perfect**, as your heavenly Father is **perfect**."*
Matthew 5:48

Notice that Jesus did not say that perfection is to be our unattainable ideal. He clearly said that we are to be perfect with the same perfection as God Himself.

Cicero seemed to have a better grip on reality…or did he?

In this chapter, we're going to find how realistic Jesus' words actually are, especially as they apply to you in your athletic performance.

DIFFERENT IDEAS OF PERFECTION

So, what is perfection? Seldom do two people get the same picture in their minds when they hear a certain word. For instance, when someone says they just bought a blue car, you picture a light blue car. Yet, the new car buyer had a dark blue in mind.

So it is with the word "perfect." One person interprets it as having absolutely no room for improvement. Another person sees it as simply meeting a preset standard, such as the .350 batting average.

JESUS' STANDARD OF PERFECTION

In the context of Matthew 5:48, where Jesus used "perfect," there is no question about His application. So, let's take a moment to capture that scene in our minds.

Jesus made His statement—*"You are to be perfect, as your heavenly Father is perfect"*—to His committed followers.

Most "religious" people in Jesus' day had one thing in common. They believed they would gain God's approval if they kept the many regulations handed down by the religious leaders. Jesus' disciples might have been caught up in that thinking, too.

It's the same as you thinking that, as a Christian athlete, you will have God's approval if you achieve the world's standard of perfection (e.g., a .350 batting average in baseball or softball, a 158.3 passer rating as a quarterback in the NFL, or a 25-point average in basketball).

Jesus set the record straight with five challenging statements. Each began with, *"You have heard that it was said..."* or *"You have heard that the ancients were told..."*

He then stated a standard of perfection commonly accepted by His listeners, which He followed with an authoritative, *"But I say to you..."*

Jesus contrasted man's way with God's way, man's perfection with God's perfection.

CONTRASTING VIEWS OF PERFECTION

Jesus' first statement, lining up with the common standard of perfection, was,

"You shall not commit murder..."
Matthew 5:21

Possibly, there were smug smiles on the faces of Jesus' disciples. They all thought themselves approved by that standard.

Jesus quickly followed with,

*"But I say to you that **everyone who is angry with his brother shall be guilty** before the court..."*
Matthew 5:22

Uh oh! Jesus burst wide open their bubble of self-righteousness. Who among them had not been angry at one time or another?

Then came the issue of morality. Jesus said,

*"You have heard that it was said, **'You shall not commit adultery...'**"*
Matthew 5:27

Okay, check, the disciples graded out well on that one, too.

Then Jesus added,

> *"But I say to you, that **everyone who looks on a woman to lust for her has committed adultery** with her already in his heart."*
> **Matthew 5:28**

Wow! Jesus was sure on target, bursting bubbles. His intention was not simply to usher in a new ethical code. Jesus was contrasting two standards of perfection, man's standard and God's standard.

LEGALISM VERSUS GODLY ATTITUDES

Man's standard of perfection deals with our legalistically carrying out the letter of the law. It has nothing to do with our attitude as we carry out the letter of the law.

However, God's standard of perfection deals with our attitudes. It is from these attitudes that our actions flow.

1. ***What is the definition of athletic perfection in this handbook?***
2. ***What difference is there between man's way and God's way in athletic performance?***
3. ***How might these two different standards affect your performance?***

GOD'S PERFECTION = GOD'S WAY

The *"perfection"* Jesus referred to in Matthew 5:48 is God's way for you to perform. It does not refer to sinless perfection. God will bring us to that amazing state after our life on earth is over, not before. Jesus referred to perfection as doing things God's way, as God Himself is the standard for perfection.

As a Christian athlete, Jesus' perfection deals with your attitudes and has nothing to do with how much mental and physical ability you have. It has nothing to do with how well you compare statistically with other athletes.

ABILITIES FOR A PURPOSE

Even so, God is concerned with the development of your athletic skills. How do we know that? Because according to **Proverbs 16:4**, He gave your abilities and enjoyment of sports to you for a purpose.

> *"The Lord has made everything for its [His] own purpose..."*

CHOICE, NOT LUCKY BREAKS

When the world hangs a label of "perfect" on an athletic performance, many factors usually fall into place that could just as well have gone the other way.

For instance, a perfect no-hit game for a baseball or softball pitcher might be the result of some "lucky breaks." Several outs could have been made by sensational fielding plays.

A perfect night at-bat might have been made possible by the late start a fielder had in attempting to get to a routine fly ball. And, of course, this is true in every sport. "Lucky breaks."

Athletic perfection by the world's standard has many factors, including "lucky breaks." But there are no "lucky breaks" in athletic perfection from God's viewpoint.

It's a matter of choice.

STARTS WITH GOD'S THOUGHTS

The first choice is to have God's thoughts. And…God's thoughts form God's actions. Now, here's an eye-opener. According to **Isaiah 55:8-9**, unless we are consciously thinking God's thoughts, we are not thinking His thoughts.

*"**For My thoughts are not your thoughts.** Neither are your ways My ways; declares the Lord. For as the heavens are higher than the earth, so are My ways higher than your ways, And My thoughts than your thoughts."*

To have God's thoughts, we must choose to have them.

Here's the thing. Our natural way of thinking and performing is not God's thoughts and actions. It isn't natural to love someone who purposely wrongs us. Just like it isn't natural to be patient under the pressure of problems. God's way isn't natural.

It's supernatural.

INTERNAL, NOT EXTERNAL

Man's standard of athletic perfection is both natural and external. For the running back in football, it might be a 150-yard per game average. For the tennis player, it might be seven aces in a match. The golfer's standard of perfection might be two putts on every green.

In man's perfection, outward results are more important than our attitudes, purpose, and motivation. Yet God tells us,

"All the ways of a man are clean in his own sight, but the Lord weighs the motives."
Proverbs 16:2

Athletic perfection, from God's viewpoint, begins on the inside, having God's thoughts. It flows inside-out from our mind to outward results that can be seen in our actions.

1. ***Why is having God's thoughts so important?***
2. ***Why is it a choice to have God's thoughts?***
3. ***To what degree have you been consciously thinking God's thoughts and performing His way in your athletic performance? Use current athletic performances to illustrate.***

ATHLETIC PERFECTION IN THIS HANDBOOK

Jesus used the word "perfect" in **Matthew 5:48**, *"You therefore must be perfect, as your heavenly Father is perfect..."* to describe someone who chooses to think God's way.

As a Christian athlete, your attitudes and thoughts are to reflect those of Jesus Christ. Your actions will then honor God because they are the physical expression of His attitudes and thoughts. With this in mind, let's put a handle on athletic perfection.

Athletic perfection in this handbook is thinking and performing God's way in union with the Spirit of Jesus Christ in you.

EACH AN OPPORTUNITY

So, your training sessions, practices, and competitions are opportunities to be perfect—thinking God's thoughts and performing His way.

God's standard of athletic perfection is not achieved by "lucky breaks." It is achieved by the Christian athlete who wants above everything else to please God.

THE SHOCKER

There is nothing you can do on your own power to think God's thoughts and perform His way. In this handbook, we are not talking about doing it God's way by your own power.

Keep in mind the words of Isaiah 55:8, "For My thoughts are not your thoughts, neither are your ways My ways; declares the Lord."

POWER FOR PERFECTION

Athletic perfection is a performance pleasing to God because it is done His way and performed by His power. The source of this power is Jesus Christ living in and through you by the Holy Spirit.

Only through the work of the Holy Spirit can these thoughts and ways be brought to your consciousness. Jesus spoke of this to His disciples a short time before He was crucified.

> *"These things I have spoken to you, while abiding with you. But the Helper,* ***the Holy Spirit, whom the Father will send in My name, He will teach you all things,*** *and bring to your remembrance all that I said to you."*
> **John 14:25-26**

1. ***God's standard for athletic perfection can only be achieved if Jesus Christ is living in you through His Holy Spirit (Romans 8:9).***
2. ***So, we will detail how that happens in the next three chapters. Are you ready? You are on the threshold of a great new athletic experience!***

SCAN FOR KINGDOM SPORTS MINUTE

SCAN FOR CHAPTER LECTURES

CHAPTER TWO

THE START OF PERFECTION

The perfect athletic performance is one you do God's way. But, to do it God's way, you need God's power. You can never experience it on your own power.

In the 1970s, the Superstars on national television were a highly popular sporting event. It featured ten top athletes from ten different sports competing in events that were not their own.

Bob Seagren, the world recorder-holder in the pole vault at the time, was its first winner, and pro soccer Hall of Famer Kyle Rote Jr. was the program's first three-time winner. Yet Kyle didn't try for a fourth title. In explaining to me why he didn't, he said:

"I didn't go for a fourth title for a combination of reasons. One of them was I had started to worry about losing. I had totally lost the perspective I had the first year when I was going down to use the gifts that God had given me to honor Him.

"I became worried about defending my title. I found myself saying, 'Wow, I've got to train to beat Bob Seagren. I've got to train to beat O.J. Simpson.' My all-consuming thought was, 'I've got to win.' Until I got that straightened out, I didn't want to compete.

In Kyle's first Superstars competition, he experienced the freedom that relying on God gave Him.

Yet, somewhere along the way, the world's idea of perfection had crept in. The highly competitive Kyle started to rely more on his own abilities than on God for whatever purpose He had in mind.

Performing God's way is empowered by God, not ourselves. And we experience God's power by yielding to Jesus Christ, whose Spirit is in each of His followers.

In this chapter, you will see how the Spirit of Christ in you (Romans 8:9) is the key to your perfect performances…doing it God's way.

On a scale of 1 to 10 (1 = not at all, 10 = extremely), how frustrated do you get when you make a mistake during competition? Explain. On a scale of 1 to 10 (1 = not at all, 10 = extremely), how focused are you on athletic perfection? Explain. Do you think it's possible to be mistake free during competition? If you answered yes, is it possible to achieve that goal throughout a game, a season, a career, etc.? Explain.

WHO YOU ARE

Just for a moment, let's focus on you. How would you say other people might describe you? "Great!" "Terrific!" "Nice!" "All right!" Hey, those words are good, but they don't say a lot, do they?

People who know you could go into detail concerning your likes and dislikes. "He likes chocolate cake and football." "She likes volleyball and hanging out with friends." That might describe you a little better.

People who know you more intimately could disclose things that might surprise you. But really, who are you? Might you be even more than how your closest friends see you?

HOW GOD SEES YOU

Only the Bible explains who you really are. You are the masterpiece of all God's creation!

> *"For you formed my inward parts; you knitted me together in my mother's womb. I praise you,* ***for I am fearfully and wonderfully made.*** *Wonderful are your works; my soul knows it very well. My frame was not hidden from you, when I was being made in secret, intricately woven in the depths of the earth. Your eyes saw my unformed substance; in your book were written, every one of them, the days that were formed for me, when as yet there was none of them."*
> **Psalms 139:13-16**

You didn't just happen by chance. The Designer of our entire universe designed you. Do you know how ridiculous it would be to think that you just happened randomly, with no design and intent from our Creator?

Let's say you have an antique watch with many delicate springs and gears. If you took the watch completely apart, put the pieces in a paper sack, shook the sack, and threw the pieces into the air, what chance do you think all the parts would have in falling back together in perfect working condition...without the aid of anyone?

You would have about the same chance of coming together without God's design and workmanship. Because of God, you are completely unique. He made you that way. And, according to **Psalms 8:3-5**, you are continually on His mind.

> *"When I look at your heavens, the work of your fingers, the moon and the stars, which you have set in place,* ***what is man that you are mindful of him, and the son of man that you care for him?"***

As unique as you are, with God always having you on His mind, it's impossible for you to enjoy close fellowship with Him on your own merit.

The Bible explains it this way:

> "...for ***all have sinned*** and fall short of the glory of God..."
> **Romans 3:23**

While there are some who always believe they are "right with God" and never sinned, they are wrong because Romans 3:23 teaches that all have sinned. They are likely counting on a divine sliding scale, or some religious ritual, but whatever their reason, most people think that on judgment day they probably come out on top. But that's not what the Bible says. Read Matthew 7:13-14. What does it say about how many inherit God's blessing after death? Read Matthew 7:22-23 where those standing before Jesus present their case. They seem certain about their right standing before God. Jesus tells them to depart from him because in reality, "he never knew them" and they still had sin on their record. What is your reaction to Jesus?

THE SIN PROBLEM

The word "sin" is an ancient archery term. It simply means "missing the mark." The "sin mark " is the distance between the bull's eye on a target and the actual place the arrow hits.

When the Bible tells us that we have sinned, it describes our missing the mark of God's perfection. Sin is falling short of God's glory—God's revealed greatness. Now that creates a problem, doesn't it? There is no possible way to fellowship with God in that condition. Just as oil cannot mix with water, God cannot mix with sin.

So, what do we mean by fellowshipping with God? Fellowship is when two or more people share things in common and participate together in those things.

For instance, players on a ball team have fellowship by sharing a team name, coaches, equipment, practices, competitions, road trips, etc. When these players share the same likes and dislikes, the bond of fellowship is even closer.

With you continually on God's mind, He wants close fellowship with you, like the fellowship He had with His Son, Jesus, when He was walking the roads of Palestine.

But we have a problem similar to what happened to All-American Roy Riegels in a New Year's Rose Bowl football game.

The 1929 Rose Bowl game was to determine the Number One team in the country. Undefeated and untied, Georgia Tech was facing the undefeated and once-tied University of California.

Disaster struck in the second quarter of a scoreless game. Stumpy Thomason, carrying the ball for Georgia Tech, fumbled when hit on his 36-yard line. Roy Riegels of California grabbed the ball mid-air and raced toward the goal line. So far, all good.

However, just as Riegels was about to be swarmed under by a host of Georgia Tech players, he planted his right foot and reversed his direction. To the surprise of everyone, he was running toward his own goal line with his teammates following, shouting, and trying desperately to stop him.

One of his teammates finally caught up to him on his own 12-yard line. However, the momentum was too great. The bewildered Riegels finally got turned around, only to have a pack of grateful Georgia Tech players bury him on the one-yard line.

California elected to punt on first down to get out of the bizarre situation.

Ironically, Riegels, playing center, snapped the ball to the player who had tried to turn him around. His kick was blocked, and Georgia Tech was given a two-point safety. Those two points proved to be the margin of victory for Georgia Tech, 8-7.

Riegels later said, when explaining how he felt, that it was difficult to grasp that he had done something so wrong.

Everyone in the Rose Bowl saw what Roy Riegels did. He made a mistake. We all make mistakes. His mistake was more obvious because of the situation. Perhaps no one noticed the missed blocks by other players in the game that had a bearing on the outcome. But they all saw number 11, an All-American, gallop the wrong way.

Riegels' sense of direction was less than perfect. However, he didn't mean to run the wrong way. Imperfect actions are simply the actions of imperfect people like…well, like everyone.

We all have fallen short of God's perfection. On our own merit, not one of us deserves to have close fellowship with Him. In our own way, we are guilty of running the wrong way in our thoughts, life, and actions, going in the opposite direction from God.

As Isaiah put it:

"All of us like sheep have gone astray. ***Each of us has turned to his own way."*** **Isaiah 53:6**

CAN'T COMPARE WITH OTHERS

Even people who compare favorably with others fall short of God's perfection. Let me illustrate.

Let's say that three athletes are trying to jump over a canyon. The first athlete runs to the edge and takes a mighty leap. He sails out about 23 feet and crashes to the bottom of the canyon.

The next really puts some "juice" into it. He doesn't want to end up like the first. He has a great takeoff. In fact, he sails out over 27 feet. He feels good that he out-jumped the first athlete. But he also crashes. Both end up at the bottom of the canyon.

Another jumper with springs strapped to his feet goes even further, but he also falls short. Yet, compared to the other two, he was better. The problem is they all fell short and ended up in the same place.

Falling short describes us all. It doesn't matter how we compare ourselves to other people. On our own merit, we fall short of God's perfection, and we cannot be in close fellowship with Him. But God did something about our predicament. He made it possible for us to fellowship with Him through His Son, Jesus.

GOD'S INCREDIBLE GIFT

"For God so loved the world, that He gave His only begotten Son, that whoever believes in Him should not perish, but have eternal life."
John 3:16

Two things had to be done for us for us to have close fellowship with God—two things we could not do for ourselves.

First, we had to be shown who God is. It's impossible to fellowship with someone we don't even know. In Jesus Christ, God made Himself known to us!

"No one has ever seen God; the only God, who is at the Father's side, he has made him known."
John 1:18

Second, our sin problem had to be resolved. An imperfect man cannot have fellowship with a perfect God. The two don't mix. But, in Jesus, God did something to change our condition in His sight.

"For our sake he made him to be sin who knew no sin, so that in him we might become the righteousness of God."
2 Corinthians 5:21

In Jesus, God gave us a new nature…His nature.

Let's say you're a multi-millionaire, and someone owes you fifty thousand dollars. He might be a very nice person, but he still owes you the money and has no way to pay you back.

You cancel his debt out of love for him and then give him fifty thousand dollars more for a new start. Now, let's bring that illustration home.

God didn't just cancel our debt when we missed the mark of His perfection. He made it possible for our complete nature to change and a whole new life to begin!

"Therefore, if anyone is in Christ, he is a new creation. The old has passed away; behold, the new has come."
2 Corinthians 5:17

Now, it would be great if you forgave someone a fifty-thousand-dollar debt and gave him an additional fifty thousand dollars for a fresh start.

It would be even greater if you adopted that person into your own family. He would have the same rights and privileges as other members of your family. He would bear your name. He would be your heir. Well, that's precisely what God did for us in Christ.

"In love he predestined us for adoption to himself as sons through Jesus Christ…"
Ephesians 1:5

God made it possible for us to fellowship with Him now and throughout all eternity! So, how did He accomplish this? Before we could have this fellowship with God, a penalty for our sins had to be paid. The apostle Paul explained how this penalty has been paid for us.

*"For the **wages of sin is death,** but the free gift of God is eternal life in Christ Jesus our Lord."*
Romans 6:23

TAKING OUR PLACE

There is nothing we can do to pay our own penalty since we're all guilty of missing the mark. It could only be paid by someone not guilty.

Even in our law system, one person sentenced to life imprisonment cannot serve a life sentence for someone else. They're both guilty, and both must pay the penalty.

However, Jesus Christ was innocent of missing the mark of His Father's perfection. He never sinned. Only He could take our place and pay our sin penalty. Here is basically what happened.

1. Our natural end is death.
2. We are powerless to pay our own sin penalty.
3. Jesus Christ, who is perfect, paid the penalty for us.
4. This penalty payment is God's gift to us.

YOUR GREATEST DECISION

God has given us the way to fellowship with Him—now and forever—but we must decide to accept what He did. In fact, we must personally accept any gift for it to be ours.

The same is true of God's gift. We must personally accept it to make it our own. Jesus paid our penalty on the cross by representing us to His Father. The payment is only applied to our sin account when we accept it by believing in Jesus.

*"For God so loved the world, that he gave his only Son, that **whoever believes in him should not perish but have eternal life.**"*
John 3:16

WHAT "BELIEVE" MEANS

In the above passage, the word "believe" does not refer to an intellectual belief. It describes what a person does when he accepts something as true. He relies upon it as a way of life.

One day, a tightrope walker walked above a roaring waterfall. Hundreds of people gathered to watch his every step. Upon his finish, they enthusiastically applauded him. Then he took a wheelbarrow across.

Again, the huge crowd gave him a tremendous ovation. He asked the people if they believed he could safely wheel a man across the waterfall. "Sure we do," they replied. Then he motioned for an enthusiastic man down front to get in the wheelbarrow. The man's eyes widened…and he left in a big hurry!

The frightened man had an intellectual belief in the tightrope walker, but there was no way he would risk his life. So, he didn't have the belief that God requires of us. To settle into the wheelbarrow.

When we have the John 3:16 kind of belief in Jesus, we are relying on Him with our life, moment by moment, as our way of life.

At one time in my life, this kind of belief in Jesus was a new concept for me. For most of my life, I thought I was a Christian. I attended church services and even served as president of my youth group.

I thought I was about as "Christian" as anyone could get when I enrolled in a theological seminary after college. But my life was no different than the lives of my non-Christian friends. That disturbed me.

I wasn't experiencing any more power in my life than they were. I had no greater peace of mind than they had. I knew many facts about Jesus, but I still didn't have a different quality in my life.

One of the speakers at a conference I attended explained that it wasn't enough simply to know and accept some facts about Jesus as true. He said that to become a Christian, a person must willfully repent of their sins and rely on Jesus Christ with his entire life. He explained that "repent" meant to change our mind and go God's way, not keep going our own way.

The speaker also explained that relying on Jesus was a practical reliance. Yes, it included relying on facts about Jesus in the Bible, but it was also relying on Him for the details of our lives.

The speaker explained that Christianity was a personal relationship with Jesus Christ. That's when I understood for the first time what it meant to believe in Jesus…to trust and rely on Him as my way of life.

I decided to change direction in my life. To turn control of my life over to Jesus and to rely on Him. After I made that commitment, I started to notice that I had a stronger desire to learn more about Jesus. The close fellowship with God I had wanted was becoming a reality.

If you haven't already done so, why not consider making this same commitment to Jesus? But first, take a moment to understand who He really is.

A GLIMPSE OF JESUS

Jesus came from Nazareth, a poorly thought of village in Galilee. A carpenter by trade, He knew what hard work, slivers in His hands, and sweat were all about.

He knew poverty and oppression first-hand. He constantly experienced prejudice; He was Jewish in a Roman-governed community.

When He taught, though He had no formal education, even those who did not agree with Him said He taught with authority.

He gave sight to the blind, healed lepers, walked on water, and raised the dead. Those who knew Him claimed His greatest work was that He changed them into new people.

He made many thought-provoking statements about Himself: "I am the way, and the truth, and the life; no one comes to the Father, but through Me…I and the Father are one…I came that they might have life and might have it abundantly" (John 14:6, 10:30, and 10:10).

There were those who didn't agree with Jesus, mainly the religious leaders. They trumped up charges against Him, spit on Him, ripped the skin off His back, beat His face beyond recognition, and then spiked Him to a cross. He hung on the cross, with shoulders dislocated, gasping for air.

At noon, total darkness came over the land. At 3 PM, He was separated from union with His Father in payment for our rebellion against God. He died!

His enemies thought they were finally rid of Him—but on the third day after His death, He rose. Later, He appeared to more than 500 people at one time! He ascended into heaven. He promised to return!

YOUR BELIEF AND A NEW YOU

Perhaps, like me, you have never understood what it means to believe in Christ. If you have not already done so, your decision to believe in Him is the most monumental you will ever make.

In making that decision, you are acknowledging that Jesus Christ is the only way to have personal fellowship with God. You are acknowledging that Jesus represented you on the cross and paid the penalty for your missing the mark of God's perfection.

Finally, you are saying that you want to repent—to change the direction of your life—and want Jesus to take control of your life. You want His thoughts to be your thoughts and His actions to be your actions.

What happens when Jesus controls your life can be explained this way. Let's say you have basketball abilities that are inferior to those of another player.

You will never be able to duplicate his talent. You can copy his training program, follow his diet, and wear his uniform, but you will never become him.

Let's say that through some miracle he enters your body. When that happens, you start to experience the fullness of his abilities. In fact, it is no longer you playing basketball. He is playing basketball through you.

So it is in the Christian experience. You can never copy the attitudes, thoughts, and actions of Jesus Christ. When you believe in Him, He lives His life through you.

It is your belief in Jesus Christ that makes you a Christian. The following prayer simply acknowledges that belief. The words are important only in that they represent your true desire. If they do, you can make this your prayer of commitment.

"Dear Father. I want to go your way, and no longer my way. Thank you for sending Jesus Christ to pay the penalty for my sin and for revealing Yourself to me through Him. I accept what You have done for me and commit myself to Him. I will rely on Jesus to live His life in and through me."

Now, if you prayed this prayer to God, the words did not make you a Christian. Your belief in Jesus Christ did. Your relationship with God, established by your belief in Jesus, can never be broken! He has put His Spirit in you (John 14:20 and Romans 8:9), and you will be in God's family throughout eternity.

Jesus said,

> *"My sheep hear My voice, and I know them, and they follow Me; and I give eternal life to them,* ***and they shall never perish; and no one shall snatch them out of My hand."***
> **John 10:27-28**

The perfect athletic performance is Jesus Christ living in you and performing through you. In our next chapter, we will begin to see how He does that.

CHAPTER THREE

THE HOLY SPIRIT OF PERFECTION

By now, you have discovered something very important in your workouts and competitions. You can't represent Jesus Christ by your own power alone.

In fact, I can almost hear you groaning, "I just have too many weaknesses!"

Well, that's true for all of us. We all have weaknesses. For some, it's a temper. For others, it's impatience… negativism…a lack of discipline, etc. They all spell one word, W-E-A-K-N-E-S-S.

Because of our weaknesses, we can easily experience defeat in our union with Jesus concerning our thoughts, attitudes, and actions. For example, consider these two hypothetical situations.

SITUATION #1

The baserunner, taking his normal lead from first base, dares a throw from the pitcher. As the pitcher makes his move toward the plate, the baserunner breaks for second base.

Teams have had little success in stopping him, and his confidence is high. The catcher snaps a perfect throw to the shortstop covering the base, but the baserunner's "educated" foot slips safely past the tag.

The shortstop, determined to jar the runner's confidence, slaps his glove on the runner's head.

Stunned, the baserunner jumps to his feet swinging. He's the same player who talked to one of his teammates in the locker room before the game about his new life in Jesus Christ.

SITUATION #2

The basketball player at the free-throw line has one shot to tie the score, which would send the game into overtime. Eight hundred fans silently cheer her on in this game against their archrival.

Two days earlier, she had told someone how peaceful the Christian life was. However, her heart beats like a drum on the line, and her legs feel like marshmallows. Lots of anxiety. No peace.

What happened to these two athletes? Weren't they supposed to be new in Christ? They're acting like their old selves.

"Therefore, if any man is in Christ, he is a new creature;
the old things [like anger and fear] have passed away; behold, new things have come."
2 Corinthians 5:17 [The added brackets are mine.]

What these two players experienced is common.

You have most likely experienced it. You really want to live the Christian life, but on the playing field and in the arena, it doesn't go as smoothly as you thought it would.

Using the baseball runner and the basketball free throw shooter as illustrations, why cannot you experience the perfect athletic performance—doing it God's way—on your own? How does Ira and Ann Yates' experience on their Texas sheep ranch relate to you as a Christian athlete?

These two athletes experienced the same frustration in their hypothetical situations that a Texas sheep rancher and his wife had experienced.

In the 1920s, Ira Yates and his wife, Ann, owned thousands of acres in West Texas. It was land on which Ira was trying to live out his dream to raise sheep.

However, the ground was so parched that he could barely grow weeds, let alone a covering of good grazing grass. To make matters worse, the rancher's financial resources were also drying up.

Attempting to bring in money, Yates asked one of the top executives of an oil company to test-drill the land for oil. At first, the executive turned him down because no oil had ever been found in West Texas.

Eventually, because of Yates' persistence, the executive gave the go-ahead, and the company began to drill. The drillers started with three consecutive disappointments.

However, on the fourth attempt, the drilling team struck a gusher that turned out to be one of the biggest oil finds in Texas history.

Can you imagine? One night, Ira and Ann Yates went to bed soaked in mental tension, struggling to pay their mounting bills. The next night, they went to bed as soon-to-be multi-millionaires.

What a difference!

MUST TAP INTO IT

During their years in financial quicksand, unknown to Ira and Ann Yates, they had far beyond the wealth they would ever need beneath the surface. They just had yet to tap into it. Consequently, they had been struggling financially.

If you are a true Christian, like Ira and Ann Yates, you have "resources under the surface" that can enable you to experience athletic perfection—doing sports God's way.

Yes, even when another athlete plays dirty against you or when you are about to shoot a free throw with the game on the line against your archrival.

JESUS PROMISED A HELPER

Jesus never planned for us to follow Him on our own. A short time before He physically left Earth, He told his followers:

> *"If you love me, you will keep my commandments. And I will ask the Father, and **he will give you another Helper, to be with you forever.**"*
> **John 14:15-16**

Jesus promised that His Father would send His disciples another Helper. Now, there are two New Testament Greek words for "another." Knowing which one Jesus used in the Gospel of John is crucial for our understanding of the "Helper."

ALLOS AND HETEROS

Allos means "another of the exact same kind," and heteros means "another of a different kind."

The first Greek word, allos, describes the relationship between two nails that are identical in size, shape, and texture and come from the same source of metal. You pound one nail into a piece of wood, then "another," or allos. The two nails are identical in every way and do the same thing.

The second Greek word for "another," heteros, would describe the relationship between a metal nail and a wooden peg. Both the nail and the peg can fasten wood together, but they are different in both their nature and their source.

It's interesting that, in Jesus' John 14:15-16 promise, the Greek word allos was used to describe the relationship between Jesus and this Helper. Two of the same. So, why was allos used?

The implication is clear. This Helper would have the same ministry as Jesus and be identical to Jesus in nature.

Okay, but who is this Helper that Jesus told his disciples about, especially as He relates to you as an athlete? To better understand who He is, let's think about the circumstances that led up to Jesus making His amazing promise.

Jesus had been telling His men that He would be leaving them very soon. Obviously, this shook them up. The disciples had come to love and rely on Jesus, and they were not sure what it would be like to continue after His death.

Knowing how helpless and alone His men must have felt at the thought of going on without Him, Jesus promised them another Helper. Interestingly, in His next breath, He called this Helper, the Spirit of truth (John 14:17). So, unlike Jesus, who was physical, this Helper would be spiritual but just as real.

Now, this Helper whom Jesus referred to and who would be with His followers is more commonly known as the Holy Spirit. He would be in Jesus' followers spiritually, just like Jesus Himself had been with them physically. The Holy Spirit would be in Jesus' disciples, not walking alongside them.

The more aware you are of the Holy Spirit's activities, the more you will appreciate His importance of convicting people of their sin (missing the mark of God's perfection).

"And He, ***when He comes, will convict the world concerning sin,*** *and righteousness, and judgment."*
John 16:8

THREE FACTS ABOUT THE HOLY SPIRIT

To better understand who the Holy Spirit is and how He can affect your entire sports experience, let's start by observing three facts about Him.

Fact One. The Holy Spirit is God, the same as Jesus, and the Father are God.

One of the great mysteries in the Bible is that God the Father, God the Son, and God the Holy Spirit are all one, having the exact same nature. Yet they are three separate individuals.

Bible scholars have called this three-in-one-God the Trinity. Although the word *Trinity* is not used in the Bible to describe God, we see evidence of the Trinity both at the very beginning of Jesus' ministry and at the very end.

As Jesus started for the banks of the Jordan River immediately after His baptism, the Holy Spirit swooped down on Him like a dove.

At that climatic moment, the voice of God the Father came out of the heavens,

"This is my beloved Son."
Matthew 3:17

All three members of the Trinity were present at this great moment in the life of Jesus! The Father's voice and the Holy Spirit descending on the Son in the river..

After Jesus' death and resurrection, He made a reference to the Trinity in instructions to His followers gathered on a mountain in Galilee:

"Go, therefore, and make disciples of all the nations, baptizing them **in the name of the Father, and the Son, and the Holy Spirit***..."*
Matthew. 28:19

It's significant that Jesus used the word "name" in a singular sense as he referred to three individuals. Again, all are one, yet three!

Now, I realize our human mind cannot fully understand how God can be three separate persons. We can no more fully understand the Trinity than we can understand that space has no boundaries or that God had no beginning. All those truths are mind-boggling, beyond our capacity to grasp. Yet they are realities.

In his writings, the apostle Paul made it clear that one God is three separate persons. He wrote:

"... You are not in the flesh, but in the ***Spirit [Holy Spirit]****, if indeed, the*
Spirit of ***God [Father]*** *is in you. But if anyone does not*
have the Spirit of ***Christ [Son]****, he does not belong to Him"*
(Romans 8:9)

Paul calls the Holy Spirit the "Spirit of God" and the "Spirit of Christ." A little spiritual algebra tells us that if A equals B, and A also equals C, then A, B, and C are all equal. So, because the Holy Spirit equals God the Father, and the Holy Spirit also equals God the Son, then all three are equal. All three are one.

Although this is a deep thought, and it is difficult to understand—for now, just keep in mind that the Holy Spirit is God, the same as Jesus and the Father are God.

Because the Holy Spirit is God, He has a will (Acts 13:2), emotions (Ephesians 4:30), and intellect (John 16:13). And He is also all-powerful (Genesis 1:2), all-knowing (1 Corinthians 2:10–11), and He is everywhere at the same time (Psalms 139:7).

Fact Two. The Holy Spirit comes to live in a person the very moment that person turns away from their old life and receives Jesus Christ as his savior, believing—relying on Him, and trusting Him as a way of life (John 1:12).

In Old Testament days, the Holy Spirit came to different people, enabling them to do a special work. Then, after the work was completed, He left them.

For example, in Judges 6:34, God wanted Gideon to lead the Jewish people into battle against the Midianites. So, the Holy Spirit came upon Gideon to give him the power to do it.

Now, here's the difference between the Holy Spirit in the Old Testament and the Holy Spirit in Jesus' followers. In the Old Testament, the Holy Spirit only temporarily strengthened selected people for special jobs. After Jesus' resurrection, the Holy Spirit permanently indwelt each follower of Jesus (John 14:20).

In confirmation of Jesus' John 14:15-16 promise, the apostle Paul wrote to Christians:

"Do you not know that you are a temple of God,
and that the ***Spirit of God dwells in you?"***
1 Corinthians 3:16

So, today, if you are a true follower of Jesus, the Holy Spirit is living in you, even as you train, practice, and compete.

Fact Three. The main ministry of the Holy Spirit is to live the life of Jesus in and through each of His followers.

That was the gist of Jesus' **John 14:15-16** promise:

"If you love me, you will keep my commandments.
And I will ask the Father, and he will give you
another Helper, to be with you forever."

Whoa..."Helper?" Doesn't the word "Helper" suggest that the Holy Spirit will simply be helping us do Jesus' works? No, not at all, and here's why.

The Greek word for "helper" is parakletos, which means to "call to one's aid." However, in some versions of the Bible, parakletos is translated as "comforter" or "advocate" rather than "helper."

For a better understanding of what a parakletos is, let's go to the highly respected Thayer's Greek Lexicon. In it, we learn that, in a legal system, the parakletos is a lawyer who comes to the aid of a person.

However, here's the twist. The lawyer comes to the aid by doing the work himself, not simply assisting his client in doing the work. In other words, the parakletos stands in for the person he represents and does all the work. That's how he helps.

As you yield to the Holy Spirit in you, He will live out Jesus' life in and through you in every aspect of your sports involvement, including your training, practices, competitions, nutrition, sleeping, mental preparation, etc.

While the phrase "yielding to the Spirit" is not explicitly mentioned in the Bible, the concept is implied. Romans 6:13 discusses surrendering to God, and Romans 6:19 talks about offering our bodies as "servants to righteousness for holiness/" This is in contrast to yielding to sin and the flesh.

Jesus taught His disciples the night before He was crucified,

"but I tell you the truth, it is to your advantage that I go away;
for if I do not go away, ***the helper shall not come to you;***
but if I go, I will send him to you."
John 16:7

Here's the thing. Jesus' work on earth was not confined to just a few short years with a small band of men. That was only the beginning! The Holy Spirit has continued Jesus' work on earth in and through His followers, and He will do the same through you in your athletics as one of His followers.

What are the three facts about the Holy Spirit? How will the Holy Spirit be your Helper in training sessions, practices, and competitions? Discuss why it makes a difference that the Holy Spirit is a person and not an impersonal force like lightening or a principle. According to Philippians 2:11, the Holy Spirit's ministry in our lives is not to bring glory to us but rather put the attention on Christ. What might this look like in your sport?

NINE CHRIST ATTITUDES

One of the most important areas of the Holy Spirit's work in expressing Jesus in and through you is in your attitudes. Paul mentions nine of these attitudes.

"But ***the fruit of the Spirit is love, joy, peace, patience, kindness,***
goodness, faithfulness, gentleness, self-control..."
Galatians 5:22-23

Athletic competition draws out natural attitudes—like anger and fear—faster than most other areas of our lives. On the other hand, athletic competition can also be one of the greatest showcases for your Christ attitudes.

Let's see how each of the nine attitudes in the fruit of the Spirit can affect your athletic performance.

Love is the first listed. Its most outstanding quality is self-sacrifice. With love comes the willingness to give completely of yourself for someone else—your coaches and teammates.

Joy is the attitude of gladness. It does not change when circumstances change because joy is grounded in confidently knowing God is in full control of all circumstances, including injuries and other setbacks.

Peace refers to a calmness as you deal with problems and challenges. With peace, you have God's perspective, even in shooting a free throw with the game on the line.

Patience refers to your slowness to react negatively even when given bad treatment by a shortstop who hits your head with the ball in his gloved hand. Instead of reacting, you're able to keep your focus.

Kindness looks for ways to help others. It's an extension of Christ's self-sacrificing love working in and through you. It's the MVP attitude of a team.

Goodness is the attitude that centers on God's values. It enables you to see people and circumstances through Jesus' eyes—which are God's eyes—to see beyond the surface to the reality that God sees.

Faithfulness is an attitude of reliability that enables your coaches and teammates to trust you. When you say something, it's as good as done.

Gentleness is the attitude of humility, empty of yourself and full of Jesus.

Self-control is Christ's attitude of mastery over natural desires and impulses. It helps develop proper training habits and protects you from influences that could distract you from God's best.

The perfect athletic performance is not one in which you try to duplicate the performance of Jesus Christ. In fact, the Christian life is doomed to frustration when we try to live it by our own power.

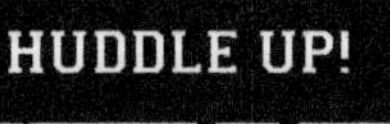

Of the nine fruits of the Spirit (Galatians 5:22-23), which two or three do you think will affect you the most as a Christian? The Bible uses the term "flesh" to refer to our sinful nature that is bent towards rebellion against God (Galatians 5:24-15). Share an example of conflicting desires of the "flesh" and the Holy Spirit in your life.

The perfect athletic performance is one in which you perform like Jesus because He is performing through you in oneness with the Holy Spirit! It is a supernatural life.

SCAN FOR
KINGDOM SPORTS MINUTE

SCAN FOR
CHAPTER LECTURES

CHAPTER FOUR
YIELDING TO THE SPIRIT

Most Christian athletes look forward to focusing on Jesus in their performances—and yielding to Him—once they learn that the Holy Spirit will live out the life of Jesus through them. They can only imagine what that would be like.

Yet, as workout follows workout and competition follows competition, many of these same athletes, out of old habits, try to experience Jesus in their performances by their own power. And, of course, they cannot successfully do that.

Consequently, these athletes fail to experience the close union with Jesus in their sports that God wants for them, and they end up frustrated by their unsuccessful attempts. Some even lose sight of the fact that the Holy Spirit really does live in them.

Knowing that the Holy Spirit lives in you is one thing. But experiencing Him living the life of Jesus in and through you is still another. To be successful, you must carry out your responsibility in your union with the Holy Spirit.

AN ATHLETE-COACH METAPHOR

Hopefully, this illustration of an athlete and coach can help you better understand your responsibility.

Let's say your coach tells you that if you place yourself totally under their authority, you will become all-conference. Now, because of your coach's promise, you have a decision, don't you?

You can choose to try to develop your skills on your own and hope for the best, or you can choose to yield to your coach and trust their promise.

Let's say a wrestler is about to attempt a double-leg take-down on his opponent. Of course, the wrestler must consciously think about that move to make it happen.

In other words, it takes a conscious effort on the wrestler's part. The double-leg take-down won't happen by itself. The wrestler remembers his coach's instructions and consciously looks for the right opening. Then, at that right moment and with his coach's instructions in mind, he makes his move.

Here's the thing. The coach gave excellent instructions. However, the coach's instructions would not have affected the wrestler's performance if the wrestler had not purposefully followed through with them.

In the same way, the Holy Spirit does not control your mind unless you are alert to His direction and yield to Him to live, through you, the life of Jesus.

The attitude and action of the baserunner and free throw shooter in the preceding chapter reveal that they were not yielding to the Holy Spirit in them.

How do we know that? Because neither their attitude nor their physical action resembled Jesus.

When we speak of habit, we are speaking of regular, frequent practices that seem almost second nature. Habits comprise about 70% of our daily activities. Before you made a commitment to do sports God's way, you likely developed some bad habits. What might be a few in training or competing? Take a look at the following verses, which can help us to understand how habits are defined in the Scriptures: Hebrews 5:13, Hebrews 10:25 and 2 Peter 2:14. It's been said that a Christian is not "plaster;" rather, the Bible says that we are clay in the hands of the Potter. Explain how this might relate to your character development in sports.

BE FILLED WITH THE SPIRIT

Being filled with the Spirit is the gist of what the apostle Paul told us we must do to experience the Holy Spirit living the life of Jesus in and through us. He wrote:

"Do not be drunk with wine, but ***be filled with the Holy Spirit."***
Ephesians 5:18

The word "filled" means "controlled." Paul was saying that, as Christians, we are to be controlled by the Holy Spirit. And we are controlled by the Holy Spirit only when we yield to Him as an athlete yields to their coach.

In this Ephesians 5:18 passage, Paul describes the "filling" of the Holy Spirit in contrast to being drunk with wine.

When a person is drunk with wine, his mind is under the influence, or control, of the wine, which produces in him staggering moves, angry outbursts, insensitivity, etc. The attitudes and actions of one who is drunk reveal the wine's influence on his mind.

So, when Paul commanded true Christians to be filled with the Spirit rather than be drunk with wine, he was commanding us to yield to the Holy Spirit, having our minds totally under the influence and control of the Holy Spirit.

The command to *"...be filled [controlled] by the Spirit..."* is written in the present tense, which means we are to be continually filled.

This filling, or control, by the Holy Spirit, is a moment-by-moment yielding as a way of life. It takes place on the football field and volleyball court in the same way it takes place at home.

THE HOLY SPIRIT AND GOD'S WORD

In the three verses following Ephesians 5:18–verses 19-21, Paul listed several actions that flow out of Christians filled with the Spirit.

Spirit-filled Christians address one another in psalms, hymns, and spiritual songs, singing and making melody to the Lord with their hearts, giving thanks to God, and submitting to one another out of reverence for Christ.

Now, lest we think we become great singers when we are filled with the Holy Spirit, let's briefly look at what these actions really mean, especially for you as a Christian athlete.

"Speaking to one another in psalms and hymns and spiritual songs, singing and making melody with your heart to the Lord..." (Ephesians 5:19) refers to the connection between the Holy Spirit and God's Word in you.

Your conversation with your teammates and coaches will be based upon God's thoughts from the Bible that the Holy Spirit impresses upon your mind.

You'll also have a gladness in your heart that others will notice.

*"**Always giving thanks** for all things in the name of*
our Lord Jesus Christ to God, even the Father..."
Ephesians 5:20

Because of the connection between God's Word and the Holy Spirit in you, you can thank the Lord in every situation, no matter how difficult.

Apart from Christ in you, it isn't easy to be genuinely thankful for a broken leg or pulled muscle, is it?

That's because we don't naturally view such things from God's perspective. The Holy Spirit will enable you to be really thankful to God as you yield to Him and rely on Him.

The phrase "...in the name of our Lord Jesus Christ" speaks of your union with Jesus. It means that it will be the Holy Spirit using your mind and voice to give thanks, just as if Jesus were physically in your situation. And, as you yield to His Spirit in you, Jesus is in your situation (Romans 8:9).

A CHALLENGING SITUATION

Perhaps you just read the starting lineup, and your name isn't on it. Your natural reaction might be disappointment, even bitterness toward your coach.

But, in the connection between God's Word and the Holy Spirit, He recalls to your mind God's thoughts:

***"And we know that God causes all things** [including not being in*
the starting lineup] to work together for good to those who love
God, to those who are called according to His purpose."
Romans 8:28

You don't know what will happen if you aren't in the starting lineup, but you keep your mind riveted on God's thoughts in the Bible and rely on Him to do whatever He chooses to do.

One way the Holy Spirit might live Jesus through you is to thank God for your situation, knowing He is working even this situation for good because of your love for Him.

Being *"subject to one another out of reverence for Christ"* (Ephesians 5:21) means that you will look out for your teammates' benefit more than your own out of your deep respect for Christ.

KNOWING YOUR "TEAM MANUAL"

In the same way, you limit your coach's influence by "listening" to them with cotton in your ears; you limit the Holy Spirit's influence by not being alert to Him speaking through the Bible.

Let's say you missed a basketball practice session when a new play was taught. You're in the game when your coach wants to run that play. There are no timeouts left, and there isn't time to ask one of your teammates what to do.

Your coach is all over you as you come to the sideline after the play fails because you did not know it.

Your coach doesn't appreciate your excuse for not being at practice and lets you know that you, as a member of the team, have a responsibility to learn from the coaching staff or your teammates what happens at missed practice sessions.

In the Christian life, you also have a responsibility to know the thoughts of God from your "team manual," the Bible.

So, how important is our knowing what God says when it comes to our yielding to the Holy Spirit in us?

THE EPHESIANS/COLOSSIANS CONNECTION

What Paul instructed the Christians in Colossae to do gives us our answer:

"Let the word of Christ dwell in you richly..."
Colossians 3:16

After those instructions, Paul listed the same actions that he listed in his letter to the Ephesians.

Yes, the exact actions come from two seemingly different commands—*"be filled with the Spirit"* in Ephesians and *"let the word of Christ dwell in you richly"* in Colossians.

Bible scholars tell us that the actions following Colossians 3:16 are the same as those following Ephesians 5:18 because Paul wrote both letters during the same week.

From a Roman prison, using different words, Paul told Christians in Ephesus and Christians in Colossae to do the same thing. To the Ephesians, Paul said to be filled, or controlled, by the Spirit. To the Colossians, he explained how to do it.

Colossians 3:16 teaches that being filled with the Holy Spirit is the same as letting the word of Christ dwell in us richly.

The Greek word for "dwell in," enoikeo, means "to inhabit" or "take up residence in, " like living in a house. Christ's words are to be as at home in us as we would be in the house in which we have lived for many years.

THE ROLE OF YOUR MIND

"We have the mind of Christ."
1 Corinthians 2:16

In Paul's letter to the Romans, he mentions the importance of our mind in experiencing the Holy Spirit living the life of Christ through us.

*"And do not be conformed to this world, **but be transformed by the renewing of your mind**, that you may prove what the will of God is, that which is good and acceptable and perfect."*
Romans 12:2

In this passage, the word "mind" refers to all of our senses, the primary organ in us being our brain.

The human mind, acting independent of the Holy Spirit, can produce great works. But it can also produce chaos. God designed your mind to work in union with His Holy Spirit, not independent of Him.

Of course, God is not limited to working through your mind. He is all-powerful and can bring about His will in many ways. But it is in your mind where the Holy Spirit engages God's Word in the Bible to express the life of Jesus in and through you.

FELLOWSHIP CAN BE BROKEN

The word "fellowship," as it's used in the Bible, refers to having mutual thoughts and interests and pursuing the same purpose with someone else. The same is true of your fellowship with God.

Sin, on the other hand, breaks this close harmony with God. And sin is in us all. It usually operates in one of two ways.

1. Sin can be a deliberate thought or action.

For instance, if you knew your coach desired you to play your position a certain way and you deliberately chose to play it your way, fellowship with your coach would be broken.

Sin is often an active rebellion against the control of the Holy Spirit. You know what God desires, but rather than yield to Him, you choose your own way. Consequently, at that moment, you miss the mark of His perfection.

2. Sin can also be the result of indifference to the Holy Spirit.

Indifference breaks fellowship with God the same way it does with your coach.

For instance, if you're daydreaming when your coach talks to you or you couldn't care less about what he/she says, your fellowship with your coach is broken.

Now, you're not actively rebelling against your coach. You're just indifferent. However, the result is the same as if you had actively rebelled against them.

Yes, you would still have a relationship with your coach. You would still be on the team, but fellowship with your coach would be broken.

And fellowship must be restored if you are to experience the maximum closeness in your relationship.

The same is true of your fellowship with God. You are still in God's family when fellowship with Him is broken, but that fellowship must be restored for you to experience maximum closeness with Him.

HOW TO MEND BROKEN FELLOWSHIP

Fortunately, God tells us how to get back into fellowship with Him:

*"**If we confess our sins,** He is faithful and righteous to forgive us our sins and to cleanse us from all unrighteousness."*
1 John 1:9

To mend broken fellowship with God, you must agree with Him that your thoughts and actions were wrong and that His way is the right way.

The word "confess" means to agree with God. But that's not all. It carries with it the implication of a strong desire to do whatever God wants you to do.

In the last chapter, our two examples show that the baserunner and free-throw shooter were out of fellowship with God, but they didn't have to remain in that condition.

By responding the way God wants them to in 1 John 1:9, fellowship could have been immediately restored…on the base path and at the free throw line.

Let's see how the two athletes could have handled it.

THE BASERUNNER

The baserunner would not have come up swinging if he had been controlled by the Holy Spirit during his attempted steal of second base. How do we know that?

One of the attitudes or results of the Holy Spirit's control of our minds is patience. In the last chapter, we learned that patience is slowness to anger even when we are given bad treatment.

The baserunner was definitely given bad treatment. Yes, the shortstop was clearly in the wrong. But the baserunner's reaction tells us that he was also wrong. He was not allowing himself to be controlled by the Holy Spirit. His response did not reflect Jesus' patience.

If the baserunner doesn't restore fellowship with God, he could still be unsettled with anger long after the incident is over. He might even try to get revenge.

At best, the baserunner will feel embarrassed in front of his teammates, some of whom might have been looking to him as a Christian example.

According to I John 1:9, the baserunner needs to agree with God that he was wrong! This agreement includes the determination to put anger out of his life forever.

Now, that doesn't mean he will never get angry again. And it certainly doesn't mean he can rid himself of anger by his own willpower. However, it does mean that he wants the Holy Spirit to live the life of Jesus through him.

The baserunner then claims God's promise in **1 John 1:9** to forgive him for the wrong that broke the fellowship totally.

"…He is faithful and righteous to forgive us our sins…"

The additional promise in this passage, that He will "…cleanse us from all unrighteousness," means He will also remove the feeling of guilt because of the sin.

We claim a promise from God simply by counting it as accurate! Take a look at 1 John 1:9 once again. John tells us that "He is faithful..."

The word "faithful" means that when God says it, we can believe it!

Now, to be clear, we are talking about restoring fellowship with God in

1 John 1:9, not entering into a relationship.

You already have a relationship with God because of Jesus Christ paying your penalty on the cross. You restore broken fellowship with Him by agreeing with Him and accepting His promise of complete restoration.

One more point. The baserunner can also acknowledge to his teammates that he "blew it." Really?

Yes, this acknowledgment will eliminate any pressure he might feel to try to live the Christian life in his own power. It can't be done, and he would be doomed to failure if he tried. Again, God designed the Christian life to only be lived in union with the Holy Spirit.

One last step for the baserunner might be to apologize to the shortstop. Sure, the shortstop was wrong, but so was the baserunner. Remember, God loves the shortstop, too.

THE FREE THROW SHOOTER

As the basketball player stood on the free throw line, she felt as if a 2000-pound boulder was weighing her down.

She knew one inaccurate move of her arms or fingers would throw the ball off course. Her rhythm was gone except for the rhythmic beat of her pounding heart.

In this situation, she can do something about it before she even shoots.

Her fears should alert her that she was playing for the wrong audience. She knows that she will let a lot of people down if she misses. She also knows she will receive big-time recognition if she makes it. Her mind is not focused on Jesus.

Remember, the Holy Spirit is always consistent with God's Word in the Bible. And God's Word tells her that she is to do everything with Jesus as her only audience. Not other people.

Paul put it this way:

"Whatever you do [including shooting a free throw in a game-deciding moment], ***do your work heartily, as for he Lord*** *[your only audience] rather than for men [people in the stands]."*
Colossians 3:23

The basketball player knows what she needs to do to restore her fellowship with God.

So, right at the free throw line, she takes a deep breath and agrees with God that she was thinking about her own welfare. Then she mentally yields her mind and body to the control of the Holy Spirit, thinks of Jesus as her only audience, relaxes, and shoots the free throw.

It's been said that attitude plus action equals glorying the Lord in sports. Explain how that might be true. We can, of course, glorify God with our words of praise and thanksgiving. We can also glorify God through our works of service for Him. Jesus said, "Let your light shine before others, that they may see your good deeds and glorify your Father in heaven" (Matthew 5:16). Bearing fruit for the kingdom of God also brings glory to Him (John 15:8). Even in our manner of death, we can glorify God (see John 21:19). What are some examples in sports where you have seen this?

FIRST REACTION

Your first reaction in any situation can tip you off as to whether you really are filled, or controlled, by the Holy Spirit.

Anger released in a temper outburst is not the work of the Spirit, and fear because of the crowd or game situation is not of the Spirit.

Jealousy, indifference to coaches, breaking training rules, and critical remarks about teammates are not of the Holy Spirit, either.

STAY ALERT

So, stay alert to your first reaction. If it is not what Jesus would do: 1) Agree with God that your attitude should be based on His Word; 2) Claim His promise in I John 1:9 that He has removed the barrier between you and Him; 3) Yield to the Holy Spirit to give you His perspective, once again, through God's thoughts in the Bible.

Remember, *"...be filled [controlled] by the Spirit..."* is a command from God. Obedience to any command from God or your coach requires a conscious choice.

THREE CHOICES

In each athletic situation, you have three choices:

1. You can choose to do things your own way.
2. You can choose to try and do things Jesus' way without yielding to the Holy Spirit.
3. You can choose to do things Jesus' way, yielding to the Holy Spirit.

The perfect athletic performance, doing it God's way, can only be experienced by the Christian athlete yielded to the Holy Spirit to live the life of Jesus in and through them.

SCAN FOR KINGDOM SPORTS MINUTE

SCAN FOR CHAPTER LECTURES

CHAPTER FIVE

THE DILEMMA

Not long after speaking to a group of athletes about how biblical principles relate to their athletic performance, I received a letter from one of the athletes who had been in attendance.

He wrote, "The most important thing I have learned is that there is a proper motivation for me as I participate in sports. Previously, without proper motivation, I was not improving. In fact, I almost quit sports altogether."

On another occasion, I sat in the office of the athletic director of a Christian college. He told me it was not unusual for outstanding athletes to enroll in his college on athletic scholarships and soon quit athletics…giving up their scholarships.

Naturally, I was curious why this phenomenon kept occurring. He explained that these athletes started to grow as Christians and were not able to relate the Christian life to their athletic performance. After struggling with their dilemma, they decided to give up athletics.

THE DILEMMA

Many Christian athletes experience something similar to this. In their union with Jesus, they experience fulfillment in their nonathletic lives. On the other hand, they have little or no awareness of Jesus in their athletic performance.

This dilemma occurs mainly in athletes who relish the recognition they receive in their sports before committing themselves to follow Jesus as their way of life. If this has been your experience, this chapter is for you.

If recognition is what drove you to endure tough drills and situations, how have you been doing in those drills and situations since you got serious about following Jesus?

You don't need that recognition from others anymore, do you? Now, you are loved and accepted by God Himself.

God Loves You

"And walk in love, as Christ loved us and gave himself up for us, a fragrant offering and sacrifice to God."
Ephesians 5:2

God Accepts You

"Therefore welcome one another as Christ has welcomed you, for the glory of God."
Romans 15:7

Ironically, instead of improving your athletic performance, it has begun to suffer. It has lessened in intensity and effectiveness. Your motivation for recognition doesn't work for you anymore.

Another factor that might be contributing to your lessened athletic effectiveness is you don't know how to be motivated by Jesus.

As a Christian, this might have even led you to question whether athletics should remain an important part of your life.

Well, relax; it's "natural" for Christian athletes experiencing this dilemma to make rationalizations during difficult training sessions or competitions. For instance, a physically exhausting drill might trigger in your mind the need to use that time for Bible study.

HUDDLE UP!

Idleness vs Idolatry

One of the most subtle — and perhaps most dangerous — forms of idleness in our training is our failure to recognize God's purposes for us when we compete is sports. We may be active in our workouts, but we have concluded that our work simply doesn't matter. On the other hand, trouble starts when our pursuit of enjoyment or influence or status in our work begins to make our work the source of ultimate satisfaction or meaning for us. When that happens, our work or how we compete has become our god. Pastor Greg Gilbert uses the illustration of driving a car. He says we must avoid the ditches of idleness and idolatry. Which of these is more challenging for you and why?

FOUR BIBLICAL FACTS

Well, let's consider four biblical facts that will help you understand how you can resolve this dilemma and experience the most effective athletic performance possible for your God-given abilities.

Fact One - A new dimension was added to your life when Jesus Christ entered.

Nothing was subtracted. Now, every athlete has at least two dimensions—the mental and the physical. If you are to reach your highest athletic potential, both of these dimensions must be fully developed. Progressively, day by day.

Your actual athletic skills are carried out through your physical dimension. However, that dimension can excel only so far as your mind, or mental dimension, drives it.

Compared to other athletes, you can be great by the full development of only those two dimensions. But you cannot become the athlete God intends you to become without the third dimension.

That third—or spiritual—dimension was added when you believed in Jesus Christ and accepted Him into your life. It is this spiritual dimension that puts you into a vital relationship with God.

Just as your mental dimension influences your physical dimension, your spiritual dimension influences your mental dimension by producing in you the attitudes of Jesus Christ (Galatians 5:22-23).

Here's the thing. When you accepted Christ, nothing was taken from your physical or mental dimensions. You gained a third—spiritual—dimension.

You have the same muscle fibers, reflex speed, coordination, etc., and the same potential brain power. But now, in your spiritual dimension, you have a direct line to the God of the universe…and His Spirit is in you.

You are now a complete, three-dimensional athlete with the capability of developing and experiencing your fullest potential.

Fact Two - God designed you with specific athletic abilities.

The Bible tells us that,

"The Lord has made everything for its own purpose..."
Proverbs 16:4

The word "everything" includes the athletic abilities God has given you. He invested certain athletic abilities in you for His purpose. Of course, in God's design, some athletes might have more abilities than you, and some might have less.

Jim Thorpe is considered to be one of the greatest athletes of all time, with an abundance of abilities. For example, in eight years of major league baseball, he compiled a lifetime batting average of .320. So, Thorpe was a great professional baseball player.

He was also an outstanding professional football player and is still regarded as one of the greatest all-around backs to have played the game.

After his playing days, Thorpe went on to become the first president of the National Football League.

Yet, there's more.

In the 1912 Olympic Games, Jim Thorpe amazed the world with his all-around athletic ability by capturing both the five-event Pentathlon and the ten-event Decathlon.

Thorpe was loaded with a wide range of amazing athletic abilities. Your abilities are most likely not as diversified as his and maybe not as amazing. Yet, God has invested in you the exact quantity and quality of abilities He wants to develop in you for His purpose.

Here's how David put it in Psalm 139 (The Living Bible):

Verse 13) *"You made all the delicate, inner parts of my body, and knit them together in my mother's womb."*

Verse 14) *"Thank you for making me so wonderfully complex! It is amazing to think about. Your workmanship is marvelous, and how well I know it."*

Verse 15) *"You were there when I was being formed in utter seclusion!"*

Verse 16) *"You saw me before I was born and scheduled each day of my life before I began to breathe. Every day was recorded in Your Book!"*

Fact Three - You have a responsibility to invest your athletic abilities for God's purpose.

In Matthew 25:14- 30, Jesus tells an interesting story about using talents. Although He was talking about money, the truth applies to any raw talent God gives you, including your athletic abilities.

In Jesus' story, three people were given varying amounts of talents, like you and your teammates, regarding athletic abilities. To one was given five talents, to another two, and to the last person, only one.

The first two people wisely invested their talents and doubled their investments. The person responsible for the one talent did not make use of it. He hoped that his Master would be pleased he didn't lose the talent, but just the opposite happened.

This was his Master's statement: "The man who uses well what he is given shall be given more, and he shall have abundance. But from the man who is unfaithful, even what little responsibility he has shall be taken away from him" (Matthew 25:29, The Living Bible).

As a Christian athlete, God has given you physical and mental abilities for a purpose. You have more than some athletes and less than others. But you do have at least one talent's worth of athletic abilities. God expects you to invest wisely in the talents you do have.

Fact Four - Your athletic abilities, along with all your other abilities, can be weapons for God's use.

From the pen of Paul:

". . . and do not go on presenting the members of your body
to sin as instruments of unrighteousness but ***present***
yourselves to God as those alive from the dead, and
your members as instruments of righteousness to God."
Romans 6:13

In this passage, the word "instruments" has the connotation of being a weapon. Have you ever thought of yourself as a weapon?

Quite a concept, isn't it? Well, that's how God wants us to see ourselves...as His weapons. The world in which we live is a battlefield for the war between God and Satan.

In his letter to the Ephesians, Paul added:

"Finally, be strong in the Lord and in the strength of His might.
Put on the full armor of God, that you may be able to stand firm
against the schemes of the devil. *For our struggle is not against*
flesh and blood, but against the rulers, against the powers, against
the world forces of this darkness, against the spiritual forces of
wickedness in the heavenly places."
Ephesians 6:10-12

In this warfare, which includes your athletics, Satan desires to control your mind, as does the Holy Spirit. That's why Paul wrote:

> *"And do not be conformed to this world, but be transformed by the renewing of your mind, that you may prove what the will of God is, that which is good and acceptable and perfect."*
> **Romans 12:2**

Weapons are instruments used to bring about victory for one side against the other. That's how God desires you to view the members of your body…again, which includes your athletic abilities…as weapons.

Since your mental dimension—or mind—controls your physical dimension, it's extremely important that the Holy Spirit in you controls your mind. Otherwise, God won't be filling you with His presence, direction, and power.

The battlefield where this war is waged between God and Satan is your home, school, athletic arena, etc. It's wherever you are.

Now, here's an eye-opener. Romans 6:13 also tells us that unless you are a weapon for God's purpose, Satan can and will use you to bring about his purpose. You are either a weapon to do God's will or Satan's will. The choice is always yours!

Which of the four biblical facts stand out to you the most? Explain.

1. ***New dimension was added to your life-Jesus***
2. ***God designed you with specific abilities.***
3. ***You have a responsibility to use your abilities for God's purposes.***
4. ***Your abilities can be weapons for Gods' use.***

COMMITMENT OF ATHLETIC ABILITIES

After understanding the preceding four biblical facts, an athlete told me, "My athletic life has not been in Christ's control. It's been my thing up until now. I want it to be Christ's from here on out. I want to give my abilities, whatever they might be, back to Him for His use."

In chapter two, you were given the opportunity to express your belief in Jesus Christ and your desire for Him to control your life.

We'll conclude this chapter with a similar opportunity for you to make a commitment to God through prayer. This time, it concerns dedicating your athletic abilities to His purpose.

Commitments are never to be taken lightly. If you desire to commit your athletic abilities, regardless of their quantity or quality, to be instruments (weapons) for God's purpose, the rest of this book is for you.

PRAYER OF COMMITMENT

Perhaps you want to make this suggested prayer your commitment:

"Lord, I realize I have been in control of my athletic ability. Right now, I give to You the complete control of the members of my body, including all of my athletic abilities. They are Yours. I commit them to be weapons for Your use. Amen!"

Your Christian life can be a true daily adventure. It can be exciting because it is the Holy Spirit living the life of Jesus in and through you. In your training sessions, in your practices, and in your competitions.

You will experience more of that new dimension and excitement in your athletic performance as you now learn how to use your abilities as God's weapons and compete for His way and for His purpose.

SCAN FOR KINGDOM SPORTS MINUTE

SCAN FOR CHAPTER LECTURES

CHAPTER SIX

THE PERFECT GOAL

PART 1

What prompted athletes in the early Olympic Games to endure painful and agonizing workouts? Was it only an olive wreath? Hardly! The olive wreath placed on a champion's head was only a symbol of the real prize.

Champions, amidst great public acclaim, received a life-time income tax exemption, their children were given a free education, and they received many other honors in their hometowns.

And today, what has athletes striving to be the best? Today the olive wreath of professional sports is the seven-figure yearly salary with fringe benefits. The amateur athlete's olive wreath used to be worldwide travel and national acclaim. Then came NIL—name, image, and likeness—and the fortune to college athletes it brought.

Athletes are willing to endure great pain if the prize is rewarding enough. To the coach's charge, "Pay the price!" the calculating athlete is thinking, "What do I get?"

Every athlete needs a goal of great value—one from which they will greatly benefit—to draw out their maximum performance. But it must be an attainable goal. Otherwise, athletes can become frustrated and lose heart. So, setting the proper goal is one of the most important things you, as an athlete, can do.

Now, finding just the perfect goal is a delicate matter. Athletes tend to set one that is either too easy to accomplish or one that is far beyond their ability. Since your athletic goal is so basic in maximizing your athletic performance, let's define what we mean by "goal."

A GOAL IS SOMETHING TOWARD WHICH YOU AIM

An archer draws his bow string and aims for the bull's-eye of the target—the small black circle in the center. As an archer, your chance of hitting it depends upon how well you aim.

In your athletic career, what you're aiming at will determine the athlete you will become. The proper goal can turn an average athlete into an outstanding athlete. However, setting athletic goals is often done with reckless abandonment, not relating to an athlete's ability.

For instance, if you set your sights below your potential, you would never fully develop your ability.

Perhaps you are impressed by the first baseman at a baseball game. Based on that impression, you decide you're going to be a major league first baseman like your hero. You go after baseball with all the enthusiasm of a hungry lion going after a piece of raw meat.

However, athletic tests reveal you would have been better suited for basketball. By aiming at the wrong goal, you have short-circuited what could have been a successful basketball career.

So, what's your goal? Perhaps you want to win the conference championship. Maybe you just want to make the team. It's safe to say that whatever your present goal is, you are not being stretched to the maximum that God has for you.

Here's the thing. Improper goals can not only prevent you from giving your best performance, but they can also leave you feeling empty and unfulfilled.

SITUATION #1

A top amateur wrestling team had its sights set on an important national tournament. Everything the wrestlers did was pointed toward that competition. It came, and they did well.

Then it happened. In the week following the tournament, each of these wrestlers started training for another important national tournament looming just two weeks away.

However, after having such a mountain-top high, they slumped into an emotional valley. Because of their letdown, they were not able to be at their emotional best for the tournament, and they did not do well.

Their team goal had lifted them to a peak for the first tournament only to drop them with a thud for the second tournament. Improper goals can do that.

Improper goals can also hinder your performance in other ways. They can tighten your reflexes, preventing you from your best performance. For example, aiming toward a long-established record.

SITUATION #2

Baseball is a sport of easy-to-compare statistics. One of the most revered is Joe DiMaggio's great 56-game hitting streak which, as of this writing, still stands.

Imagine yourself as having hit safely in 20 straight games. Your eyes are on DiMaggio's record. You're taking your final turn at bat in the very next game. You have walked twice and flown out once. Feeling any pressure? Maybe a little, right?

Okay, let's extend your hitting streak to 50 games with the same situation in the 51st game. Now, how's the pressure? You are so close to the record, yet so very far! Chances are your swing would be a little tighter than if you were just taking your natural cut at the ball.

DANGERS OF SELF-SATISFYING GOALS

An improper goal always hinders your maximum development. So, what's the main characteristic of an improper goal? One that is designed to give you personal satisfaction. Self-satisfying goals are improper goals.

One of the more common improper or self-satisfying goals is the conference championship. Let's say that you set the conference championship as your goal because you want to receive recognition as the champion. Being a conference champion would stroke your ego.

One of the dangers of a self-satisfying goal is that when the going gets tough, through pain and exhaustion, your natural, self-satisfying, tendency is to ease up, or even quit.

Easing up brings you immediate satisfaction. Although you would eventually get personal recognition as a conference champion, you will immediately get personal relief when you ease up. Both the championship and easing up bring self-satisfaction. Whichever drive is stronger in the present moment will affect your performance.

In the heat of practice and competition, relief from pain and exhaustion can momentarily overshadow the satisfaction you would eventually get as the conference champion. Your maximum athletic development is delayed in that moment of easing up…which means your maximum performance has been dialed down.

As a basketball player, you've just completed the main part of your practice and you feel drained. Then you hear your coach, "Line up for 12 all-out wind sprints! Remember the championship!"

"Oh no," you mutter, "it's puke time again!"

At this point, you aren't thinking about the championship, are you? Maybe after a shower you'll think differently, but that won't help with the wind sprints staring at you. You just want to collapse into a swimming pool.

At that moment, that would bring more satisfaction than being named "athlete of the year." The bottom line? If your heart is not in the wind sprints, you won't receive the maximum benefit. Your self-satisfying goal has stifled your present training.

Only one goal can release a Christian athlete's potential in every practice and training session, as well as in every competition. Only one goal can make you desire to run wind sprints with an all-out effort when your body screams for relief. It is not a self-satisfying goal, although there is much satisfaction involved.

THE ULTIMATE GOAL

Here's what makes that one goal the perfect goal. It focuses you on God rather than yourself.

God's athletic goal for you, as you have Jesus in your mind, is to conform you to Jesus' inner likeness in your athletic performance.

I shared this perfect goal with a distance runner of national caliber. At first, he thought it sounded ridiculous. He couldn't see any possible connection between becoming the best distance runner in the nation, which he wanted to be, and being conformed to the likeness of Jesus Christ.

And he was right! Chances are he might not have had the ability to become the best distance runner in the land. However, there is a connection between him becoming the best distance runner he could become and God conforming him to the likeness of Jesus Christ…whose Spirit was in Him (Romans 8:9).

We talked for a while, and he was willing to try it. Weeks later, he told me that, as he focused on Jesus in his training, his running had become more fun. And…he cut over 45 seconds from his BEST time in the six-mile run within a 30-day span.

Did he suddenly get more ability? No. God just released in him the ability he already had. This Christian runner had become convinced that God's goal was far superior to any goal he had ever set.

So, let's bring this back to you. You might never win a conference championship as you focus on Jesus, yielding to God conforming you to Jesus' likeness. The truth is you might not have that ability. God's perfect goal for you will not lift you beyond your ability. However, it will enable you to maximize your ability. And, of course, that could include a championship.

My distance runner friend summed it up when he said, "Great times and honors might come as a result of being conformed to the likeness of Christ, but they should never be an end in themselves."

HUDDLE UP!

1. *Define what is meant by the term "goal" relating it to your athletic performance.*
2. *What have been some of the results from setting improper goals?*
3. *What is the danger of setting self-satisfying goals for your athletic performance?*
4. *What is God's only goal for you as an athlete? Where is this found in the Bible?*
5. *Why should our focus be on the return of Christ? How can this affect your athletic performance?*

BIBLICAL PREMISE FOR GOD'S PERFECT GOAL

"For whom He foreknew, He also predestined to ***become conformed to the image of His Son****, that He might be the first-born among many brethren."*
Romans 8:29

God desires you to become just like Jesus.

Sounds incredible, right?

Now, this is a continuous process of development that will one day reach fulfillment. That's right, there is coming a day when you WILL be like Jesus. Think about that.

You will share in Jesus' glory and be in His very presence. It will be different from the pains, exhaustion, misunderstandings, and shortcomings you now experience in your training, practices, and competitions. It will be a reality you will experience. Here's how Paul described it.

"Behold, I tell you a mystery; we shall not all sleep, but we shall be changed [to His likeness], in a moment, in the twinkling of an eye [the fastest possible measure of time], at the last trumpet; for the trumpet will sound [marks the return of Jesus to earth], and the dead will be raised imperishable, and ***we shall be changed****."*
I Corinthians 15:51-52

Not only is this day coming, but God has given us the responsibility to spend more time thinking about it than we would any upcoming competition. In fact, God has commanded us to make that historic event the umbrella theme of our thought life. Everything else is to come under it. Peter made that clear for us:

> *"Therefore, gird your minds for action [having your mind controlled by the Holy Spirit], keep sober in spirit [being sensitive to the Holy Spirit's guidance], **fix your hope [attention] completely on the grace [divine love] to be brought to you at the revelation [actual appearance] of Jesus Christ.**"*
> **I Peter 1:13**

It's so unnatural to think about this great event, isn't it? We've got too many other things on our minds. Yet, look at what's in store for you by making this your disciplined practice.

> *"Beloved, now we are children of God. And it has not appeared as yet what we shall be. We know that when He appears we shall be like Him, because we shall see Him just as He is. And everyone who has this hope fixed on Him **purifies himself just as He is pure.**"*
> **I John 3:2-3**

Focusing on the very presence of Jesus will fill your mind with new attitudes. That's the purity about which John wrote. Pure attitudes are the building blocks for pure actions. It was the pure attitude of total dependence on His Father that brought Jesus through physical torment that would have stopped other men in the starting blocks.

> *"**. . . for the joy set before Him** [His attitude of wanting to please His Father above everything else] **endured the cross, despising the shame, and has sat down at the right hand of the throne of God,**"*
> **Hebrews 12:2**

You will never be able to duplicate the actions of Jesus in your athletic performance on your own. Only the Holy Spirit in you can duplicate the performance of Jesus through you.

"I just don't believe God wants me to be so unhappy. Surely, he would want me to play college basketball even if it meant cheating to accomplish it." Too many athletes believe something like this—the goal of life is personal happiness. There is often a nonstop quest in sports to win a bigger prize, no matter the cost. However, King Solomon, a man who indulged in the pursuit of happiness to the max, finally realized it was only striving after the wind (Ecclesiastes 1:14-18). He concluded the goal of life is God's glory, as taught in the Westminster Catechism. Question 1: What is the chief and highest of man? Answer: Man's chief and highest end is to glorify God and fully enjoy Him forever. Read 1 Corinthians 7:23. How does this Bible verse help the Christian athlete understand his or her ultimate goal?

Most goals athletes set for themselves are self-satisfying. And, because they are self-satisfying, they can never consistently stretch you to your maximum. In various situations, your self-satisfying goal will give way to your most immediate self-satisfying tendency. Most of the time this means you will ease up to some degree. Your self-satisfying goal has "sold you out!"

The only goal that can release you, as a Christ-Follower, to your maximum, moment by moment, is the one God has for you to pursue. Your goal is to focus on Jesus and His attitude in your situation and mentally yield to God to form in you the inner likeness of Jesus, allowing Him to express Himself through you. Even in a rehab room.

SCAN FOR
KINGDOM SPORTS MINUTE

SCAN FOR
CHAPTER LECTURES

CHAPTER SIX

THE PERFECT GOAL
PART 2

GOD'S GOAL FOR YOU WILL DEVELOP YOUR POTENTIAL

Now, let's return to those 12 wind sprints on the basketball court. Everything is physically the same, and you're still totally wiped out. However, there are two differences.

First, your goal is to focus on Jesus in running the wind sprints, yielding to God to conform you to the likeness of Jesus. In pursuing that goal, you have in mind the day you will be with Him…and like Him.

With Jesus in mind, you might end up crawling the last few sprints, but even that would be as fast as you could possibly crawl.

At that moment on the court, your opportunity to focus on Jesus and be conformed to His likeness is in running the wind sprints. Later it will be in doing something else, such as spending time with your family or studying.

God's goal for you is neither too easy nor out of reach. You'll achieve it whenever you set your mind on Jesus and the attitude He wants to express through you, yielding to God in conforming you to Jesus' likeness.

The more time you spend reading about Jesus, the better you will know Him. Similarly, in developing any friendship, the more time you spend communicating with a person, the better you will know them.

Of course, you have an advantage with Jesus that you don't have with other people. As you keep getting to know Jesus better and better, the Holy Spirit will recall to your mind His thoughts.

In fact, as you read about Jesus in His biographies (Matthew, Mark, Luke and John), the Holy Spirit will be at work exchanging your mind with His mind: "…we have the mind of Christ" (1 Corinthians 2:16).

WHAT ABOUT INTERMEDIATE GOALS?

An elite Christian athlete told me, "I understand that my ultimate goal is to be conformed to the likeness of Jesus Christ." Then he asked, "But can't I have an intermediate goal, such as the Olympic Games? There's nothing in the Bible that says I can't, is there?"

Before I explain how I answered him, let me clarify what he meant by "intermediate goal." An intermediate goal is something toward which you aim that will draw you closer to your ultimate goal. It's a step along the way.

Since this athlete's ultimate goal was to be conformed to the likeness of Jesus, any valid intermediate goal would have to draw him closer to Jesus' likeness. If it didn't, it would not be a valid intermediate goal.

In answering him, I said, "Olympic Games, league championships, personal honors, specific distances, and times, etc., are not legitimate intermediate goals. In themselves, they don't help you become like Jesus Christ in your athletic performance."

However, let's ask the Christian athlete a different question: "If my only goal is to focus on Jesus and be conformed to His likeness, is there a place for events like the Olympics, conference playoffs, etc., in my planning?"

Yes, there is! Even though they are not legitimate intermediate goals since they don't directly conform you to the likeness of Jesus Christ, there is a place for them in your planning if you have the ability to make training for them realistic.

Keep in mind that there is a Grand Canyon-size difference between striving for the Olympics and other personal honors and simply experiencing them as a result of your ability. Olympic tryouts, league play-offs, and pro tryouts are events that can be scheduled on a calendar and be part of your training program for peaking at the right time.

Interestingly, God has given us information on how to look upon specific events that are geared to a time schedule.

"Come now you who say today or tomorrow we shall go to such and such a city and spend a year there and engage in business and make a profit. ***Yet you do not know what your life will be like tomorrow. You're just a vapor that appears for a little while and then vanishes away.*** *Instead, you ought to say, 'If the Lord wills, we shall do this and do that.'"*

James 4:13-15

An athletic paraphrase of this passage could be: "Come now, you who say next year I shall make the Olympic team and achieve a specific performance. Yet you do not know God's intent for your athletic talent. You're just a vapor that appears for a little while and then vanishes away. Instead, you ought to say, 'If the Lord has designed my being in the Olympics as part of His plan for my life, I shall make the team by peaking for it.'"

It is biblical to plan your workouts for a peak performance for specific events, whether they be the Olympic tryouts, league play-offs or some other specific competition. However, it is not biblical to drive toward such events as either your ultimate or intermediate goal. If you do, you might be putting your energies into something that God doesn't want for your athletic career…and missing out on what He does want.

Although such events are not to be your goal, God might still want you to experience them for a purpose He has in mind. So, there's nothing wrong with planning your training program to peak for a scheduled event. It becomes wrong only when you allow it to take your mind off your ultimate athletic goal of focusing on Jesus and yielding to God to conform you to the likeness of Jesus.

Now, keeping the right balance can be difficult. Jesus warned us of the danger of striving toward God's purpose while pursuing something else from our own desires, such as the Olympics. Jesus put it this way:

"No man can serve two masters, *for either he will hate the one and love the other, or he will hold to one and despise the other.* ***You cannot serve God and mammon."***

Matthew 6:24

"Mammon" refers to anything that is not of God, usually of a material nature. Jesus was referring to a person trying to do things God's way while having desires not from God. It's impossible to serve God and yourself at the same time. Jesus could just as well have been referring to you wanting to be like Jesus while, at the same time, peaking for a certain event.

Because the certain event will bring you pleasure, you can easily find your thoughts focusing more on the event than on Jesus. What started as just another event, in your overall program ended as your true athletic goal. In other words, for you, the event had become "mammon."

HUDDLE UP!

Kent Hughes, in his excellent book "The Disciplines of a Godly Man," refers to spiritual sweat as the way believers develop their full spiritual potential. He says, "We will never get anywhere in life without discipline, be it in the arts, business, athletics, or academics. This is doubly so in spiritual matters. None of us naturally seeks after God, none is inherently righteous, none instinctively does good (Romans 3:9-18). Therefore, as children of grace, our spiritual discipline is everything, everything! I repeat . . . discipline is everything!"

1. How does his statement impact your development as an athlete?

2. Read 1 Timothy 4:7, 8 Practically, what does this mean you should do? What things are holding you back in your walk with God?

3. Is there a cost to spiritual discipline? Read 1 Corinthians 9:25-27.

HOW TO KEEP YOUR EYES ON GOD'S GOAL FOR YOU

One way to remember God's goal is to mentally review it before each practice session and competition. Your goal is to focus on Jesus and yield to God, who will conform you to the likeness of Jesus in your attitudes and actions.

Your goal is not to improve your performance! Most likely it will improve. However, the improvement will be the result of maximizing your abilities as God conforms you to the likeness of Jesus.

As you focus on Jesus, you can think of your practice sessions and competitions two ways:

1. As an opportunity for God to do whatever He chooses.

Let's say that placing first will earn you a spot on a national team that will travel to Europe. You have never been to Europe, and you would really enjoy this trip. You're in second place, and the athlete in first place has already finished. It all comes down to your last effort. Unfortunately, you fall just short. Goodbye Europe!

What's your initial reaction? If you had your sights set on that trip to Europe, you would be drowning in disappointment. Yet, if your only goal were to focus on Jesus and yield to God, conforming you to the likeness of Jesus, you would see this as an opportunity for God to work His purpose.

*"**And we know that God causes all things** [even a second-place finish] to work together for good to those who love God, to those who are called according to His purpose."*
Romans 8:28

God is never stymied by circumstances. If He wanted you in Europe, He could have given you the extra effort you needed.

Here's the thing. God either causes or allows things to happen for His purpose. He is never surprised by the results. A professional football player summed it up best when he said, "When I give my all for Him, the results will be His best for me."

Although God's purpose might not be clear right away, each of your performances is simply an opportunity for God to do whatever He chooses.

2. As a two-way evaluator.

First, each practice and competition will let you know to what degree you really are performing like Jesus with His attitudes and actions.

Remember, it's impossible to be an exact copy of Jesus. You will only experience this conforming process as you consciously allow the Holy Spirit to do it through you.

Let's say you are an outside hitter in volleyball. You want to perform like Jesus, but every now and then, you relish the recognition you'll get for making a spectacular hit. On one outstanding hit, the thought flashed into your mind that the team was lucky to have you.

That unChristlike thought let you know you weren't focusing on Jesus in making the hit...and possibly haven't been many moments before it.

So, do you let that failure stifle you from pursuing your goal for the rest of the game? No, of course not. But how do you get back on track?

In **1 John 1:9**, God tells us:

*"**If we confess our sins,** he is faithful and just to forgive us our sins and to cleanse us from all unrighteousness."*

According to this passage, you sincerely agree with God that you were wrong and accept His sincere forgiveness. Then, set your mind back on Jesus and God's goal of conforming you to the likeness of Jesus...and move on!

Second, practice sessions and competitions evaluate you physically. You will not always be at the same physical level of performance due to fatigue, a variance in nutrition, injuries, etc. A careful analysis of your physical status can help avoid the pitfall of over training, which is common to many athletes.

USING FOCAL POINTS

In learning a new approach to athletics, it can help to use reminders.

DISTRACTIONS AND GOD'S INSTRUCTIONS

Interestingly, the Israelites in the Old Testament had the same problem Christian athletes can have today. The Israelites would go for a long time without even thinking about God. Like, today, in the heat of competition, it can be easy to lose your focus on Jesus and revert to your old way.

So, to help His people think about Him more consistently and go His way instead of their natural way, God instructed the Israelites to use reminders:

"Speak to the people of Israel, and tell them to make tassels on the corners of their garments throughout their generations, and to put a cord of blue on the tassel of each corner. And it shall be a tassel for you to look at and remember all the commandments of the Lord, to do them, not to follow after your own heart and your own eyes, which you are inclined to whore after" (Numbers 15:38-39).

LIVING OUT GOD'S INSTRUCTIONS

God's instructions were for the Israelites to attach tassels to the bottom of their robe with a blue cord to remind them to think about Him during their activities, and to go His way rather than their own way. To focus on Him.

You can do the same to help you remember to focus on Jesus in your training sessions, practices, and competitions. No, not using tassels, but using anything that can focus you on Jesus when you see, hear, or feel it.

For example, when Hall of Fame offensive lineman, John Hannah, played for the New England Patriots, he used the goal posts at both ends of the field. The vertical posts and cross bar represented to him the cross. So, each time Hannah lined up for a play, the goal post reminded him to focus on Jesus for that play, and to sacrifice himself for the team by going all out.

Your focal point might be hearing the blast of a whistle, or a cross tied to your shoe, or the voice of your coach, or a point scored, or your feeling of fatigue, or the word "Focus" printed on your hand, or…well, you get the idea.

A focal point can be anything that when you see, hear, or feel it, you focus on Jesus and yield to the Holy Spirit to express Jesus in and through you at that moment.

1. *On a scale of 1-10, how would you rate your overall focus (1 being extremely unfocused, 10 being highly focused)?*
2. *What are some areas in which you have less focus? What about some areas in which you have more focus? Can you explain why?*
3. *What are the most prominent things on your mind during competition? Do you find it easy or difficult to think about Christ or think about giving God glory?*
4. *How do you think having a Kingdom mindset (focusing on His glory) might impact the way that compete?*
5. *What are some focal points you can start using to help keep your mind on Christ during competition?*

ONE IMPACT OF THE PERFECT GOAL

Football player Kamryn Babb came to Ohio State University as a highly recruited five-star wide receiver, but he suffered one season-ending injury after another, season after season. Two torn ACLs in each knee and six total surgeries.

As a committed Christian, despite the difficulties, Babb kept his focus on Jesus, yielding to God to conform him to Jesus' likeness. He was determined to work hard at rehab while encouraging his teammates. Along the way, he introduced some of them to the Jesus he was following.

Babb's teammates elected him as one of their captains even though he had not been able to play.

On November 12, 2022, Babb was cleared to play in the final home game of his college career, against Indiana. The stadium was packed with fans who had read Babb's story of commitment and wondered if he would get in the game.

Then it happened. The fans cheered as Babb, wearing the honored zero on his jersey, trotted out to join his welcoming teammates in the huddle. Immediately, quarterback C.J. Stroud, in cahoots with coach Ryan Day, called Babb's play.

With his focus on Jesus, Babb ran his pattern with perfection and Stroud hit him in the end zone for and eight-yard touchdown...the only catch of Babb's entire college career.

Gripping the ball, Babb slumped to his scarred knees, thanking God for what had just happened. The stadium exploded with sonic level cheering, and the entire Ohio State team swarmed Babb in the end zone, with Stroud the first there embracing his Bible study buddy. Players, reporters, and fans alike said it was the most special moment of the year!

After the game, Babb and Stroud fielded questions from the press, and even hardened reporters asked them questions about their faith in God.

God's perfect goal doesn't guarantee championships or even electrifying moments like Kamryn Babb experienced. But it does guarantee that God will accomplish His purpose.

A FINAL WORD...AND REMINDER

Most goals athletes set for themselves are self-satisfying. And, because they are self-satisfying, they can never consistently stretch you to your maximum. In various situations, your self-satisfying goal will give way to your most immediate self-satisfying tendency. Most of the time this means you will ease up to some degree. Your self-satisfying goal has "sold you out!"

The only goal that can release you, as a Christ-Follower, to your maximum, moment by moment, is the one God has for you to pursue. Your goal is to focus on Jesus and His attitude in your situation and mentally yield to God to form in you the inner likeness of Jesus, allowing Him to express Himself through you. Even in a rehab room.

And keep this in mind. The more you think about the day when you will be in Jesus' presence, the more you will desire this conforming process to take place in your athletic performance.

CHAPTER SEVEN

PERFECT WINNING

In this chapter, we will get a biblical definition of winning that goes with our biblical goal. We are talking about a definition that will pull the best out of you regardless of your circumstances. However, before we do that, let's see how an improper—or unbiblical—goal, with its corresponding improper—or unbiblical—definition of winning can hinder your performance.

I asked my good friend, Gordon Thiessen—who played football for the University of Nebraska as a defensive end—to share an experience he had playing high school football. In his words:

"When I was playing on the high school sophomore football team, our defensive unit set a goal to go all season without being scored on. We called ourselves the "Zero Defense." We even made up a chant and put a "0" on our helmets.

"Things went just like we wanted them to go for the first nine games of the season. We shut out everyone and felt confident we would do the same for our tenth and final opponent. They had been beaten by teams that we had beaten badly.

"In the first four minutes of that last game, our offense made a mistake which gave the other team good field position. They went on to score the first touchdown that had been scored against us all season.

"It was really something. After they scored, our defense fell apart. We completely let up because we knew we could not achieve our goal of a scoreless season. They ended up beating us 44-0!"

Obviously, Gordon's defensive team didn't suddenly lose its ability after their weaker opponent scored because of a mistake by the offense. But attitude drives action and the attitude of the defense changed…because of an improper goal and its related improper definition of winning. The team's goal and corresponding definition of winning was completely circumstance-based.

Now, let's see what God's definition of winning is and how it will free you to consistently perform at your maximum.

COMMON DEFINITION HINDERS YOUR PERFORMANCE

Of course, the most widely accepted definition of winning is to "defeat your opponent." Gordon's team thought that if they achieved their goal of Zero Defense, they would win by defeating their opponent. That definition relates to the common goal of defeating your opponent. Now, if we turn 180 degrees, the common definition of losing is "being defeated by your opponent."

These definitions of winning and losing have been ingrained in us from childhood. Every time we read a sports page or hear the results of recently played contests on radio and TV, we come across this definition of winning and losing. Almost every newspaper has a "win-loss" column in the sports section.

This statistical way of measuring the effectiveness of an athlete or team helps to ingrain in us this widely accepted definition of winning and losing. Lots of ink goes to the athlete who defeats the rest of the field. Not much to the defeated.

In the following two hypothetical situations, you'll see how these common definitions of winning and losing can hinder your athletic performance.

SITUATION #1

You are part of a team practicing for an opponent that has not been having a good season in what many consider to be a meaningless competition. Your team has been enjoying a very successful season. There is no doubt in anyone's mind that you are the better team. How would you and your teammates practice for the upcoming competition?

- **Practice just as intensely as if we were going up against a tough opponent for the conference championship.**
- **Be less intense in preparing for this competition.**

You know your team can lay off the whole week and still beat your opponent. If your definition of winning is to "defeat your opponent," and that's all you are practicing for, chances are great that you and your teammates won't be intently preparing for this competition. Keep in mind that athletic ability is only fully developed by maximizing each training session and practice, not by letting up when the opponent isn't a threat.

SITUATION #2

Imagine yourself well behind against an opponent who is not only stronger and faster than you but also has superior techniques. What would be your attitude in what appears to be a hopeless situation?

- **Great desire to keep mentally and physically going all-out.**
- **Lessened desire to go all out.**

Proverbs 23:7 gives us insight as to what your actions would be if you were mentally letting up: *"For as he thinks within himself, so he is."* This means what you have in your mind will eventually surface in your actions. If you slacken your mental intensity, your physical actions will show it.

You're capable of releasing more of yourself, but you don't because you have no hope of defeating your opponent. Again, the common definition of winning has allowed circumstances to dictate how much of your ability will be released.

The Bible gives God's perspective on winning and losing, which is different from that of the world. As you make His perspective yours, you will be free to always do your best, even in routine training and practices.

Any definition of winning and losing must be related to your goal. If your goal is to defeat your opponent, then winning is defeating your opponent, and losing is being defeated by your opponent.

However, as we learned in our last chapter, the perfect goal for a Christian athlete is:

Focus on Jesus and yield to God to conform you to the likeness of Jesus. So, we must now have a new definition of winning, one that will draw out the best in you all the time, regardless of your opponent.

GOD'S DEFINITION OF WINNING AND LOSING

Winning is having a total release focus on Jesus Christ and yielding to God to conform you to the likeness of Jesus in each situation.

Losing is not having a total release focus on Jesus Christ.

There is a big difference from the long-ingrained definition of winning and losing, right? When you practice and compete with God's definitions of winning and losing in mind, circumstances will not control your athletic performance.

Three Bible passages give us the building blocks upon which God's perspective is based.

BUILDING BLOCK ONE

"Whatever you do, do your work heartily as for the Lord rather than for men." **Colossians 3:23**

The word "whatever" includes everything you do in your athletic performance, whether it is running, throwing, jumping, hitting, etc. The word "heartily" means you do it by totally releasing all your abilities toward the task at hand. It involves much more than just your strength.

For instance, if you were a golfer readying to make a two-foot putt, you would be leaving your mental abilities behind if you pulled back your putter and drove the ball with all your strength.

"Heartily" refers to your mental and physical abilities as well as your emotional energies. If you are a baseball player and hit away with the bunt sign on you would not be totally releasing yourself, even if you did get a hit. Obedience, concentration, reflex action, strength, speed, strategy, and enthusiasm are all wrapped up in the word "heartily."

Now, if we were to stop at this point, it would sound pretty much like the philosophy, "Just give it all you've got, and you're a winner!" But we're not going to stop here because God doesn't.

It is not just a matter of "giving it all you've got!" It's yielding to God to conform you to the likeness of Jesus as you focus on the Lord. Jesus Christ is your only audience! We so often perform for other people, fans, coaches, scouts, TV cameras, etc. We want their approval.

When the bleachers are filled with people, or a certain person is there, most athletes can really give of themselves. It all depends on how much the recognition of others means to the competing athlete. But what happens when only a few people come to see the competition? What happens if that certain person isn't there? Some enthusiasm is gone, isn't it? We are oriented toward a human audience to the point it can stifle our athletic performance if the crowd isn't large enough or if that certain person isn't there.

Well, try this. Mentally picture Jesus Christ as the only one in the stands. That's how God wants you to perform. He wants you to focus on Jesus Christ as your only audience. What a thrill it would be to perform only for Him. Colossians 3:23 says that whatever you're doing in your athletic performance, do it with your total release focus on Jesus.

BUILDING BLOCK TWO

"And whatever you do in word or deed, do all in the name of the Lord Jesus..."
Colossians 3:17

Again, we have the phrase "whatever you do." And again, it includes everything you do as an athlete. How are you to do it? Do it all "in the name of the Lord Jesus."

"In the name of the Lord Jesus" means you are to be in sync with Jesus so that you will say and do only those things He would say and do. It means you are to allow His Spirit in you (Romans 8:9) to express His attitude through you in everything you do in your athletic performance.

You can see how important it is to get to know Jesus from the pages of the Bible. Without knowing Him, you won't experience God consistently forming Jesus' attitudes, words, and actions in and through you.

BUILDING BLOCK THREE

"Therefore, we are ambassadors for Christ, as though God were entreating through us..."
2 Corinthians 5:20

An ambassador represents another person or organization. As an ambassador for Jesus, the idea is that when someone sees you, they are to see the Jesus in you. In fact, the phrase, "as though God were entreating through us..." unlocks the idea of how people see Jesus when they see you. They see God active in and through you.

The apostle John explains that God, the Creator of the universe, lives in us:

*"In that day you will **know that I am in my Father, and you in me, and I in you.**"*
John 14:20

In your oneness with Jesus, God will be expressing Himself through you as He did through Jesus while He was walking the roads of Palestine (John 14:9). In practices and competitions, think of God Himself using the abilities He has given you for a purpose He has in mind. With that mindset, even routine volleyball practice is like playing in the Olympics.

Now, let's get the full flavor of God's definition of winning by putting our three building blocks together in an athletic paraphrase.

In the likeness of Christ, as His personal ambassador (2 Corinthians 5:20) and in union with Him (Colossians 3:17), God will express Himself through you, totally releasing your mental and physical abilities as well as your emotional energies (Colossians 3:23) toward the present task.

A BIBLICAL EXAMPLE OF GOD'S DEFINITION OF LOSING

God's biblical definition of losing is based on a historic event in the early Christian church. It was a time when Christians, in an act of love, were selling their possessions and pooling the money to benefit other Christians in need.

*"But a certain man named Ananias and his wife Sapphira sold a piece of property, and kept back some of the price for himself (with his wife's full knowledge). And bringing a portion of it, he laid it at the apostles' feet. But Peter said, '**Ananias, why has Satan filled your heart to lie to the Holy Spirit, and to keep back some of the price of the land? While it remained unsold, did it not remain your own? And after it was sold, was it not under your control? Why is it that you have conceived this deed in your heart? You have not lied to men, but to God.**'"*

Acts 5:1-4

Ananias and his wife had decided to sell all their land but to give only a portion of it to the Church. Of course, it was their right to hold back some money for their own benefit. That wasn't the problem. They made a serious mistake in claiming it was the full amount when they gave it. Ananias and his wife tried to fake it.

Now, this should be a real eye-opener since athletes tend to do the same thing. When was the last time you didn't really put all you had into your athletic performance?

Often, our natural tendency is to hold back even before we feel fatigued and pain. We can fake it with other people, but we can never fake it with God. There is no way you can perform in a mental union with Jesus without having a total release focus on Him, yielding to God to conform you to the likeness of Jesus in your attitudes, thoughts, and actions.

Jesus always had a total release focus on His Father, whether He was teaching, counseling, calming a storm, or being crucified. He wanted only to please His Father and do His will!

You can defeat your opponent 50 to 1, setting a record in the process, and still be a loser from God's perspective. Neither the score nor your circumstances have anything to do with winning or losing.

HUDDLE UP!

1. ***How do you think the world's definition of winning and losing may have hindered your athletic performance?***
2. ***How has God's definition of winning and losing helped your athletic performance?***
3. ***What do you think it looks like to have a total release of your abilities while competing for God and not men?***
4. ***How close do you feel like you've come to achieving a total release of your abilities?***
5. ***What are some things that might be holding you back from doing so?***

A WINNING PERFORMANCE BY JESUS CHRIST

God has not only defined winning, but Jesus has demonstrated winning from God's perspective. Let's take a glimpse of Him in action in the Garden of Gethsemane. The setting is shortly before Jesus was taken to the cross to undergo a torturous death by crucifixion.

At approximately 11 o'clock in the evening, Jesus and 11 of His men made their way to the Garden of Gethsemane, a popular spot at the base of the Mount of Olives. Jesus left eight of His men at the garden entrance, taking three of them with Him toward the center. After leaving the three and going a little further, He slumped to the ground in agony. It was in the cool of the evening yet sweat was pouring off His body. As Jesus was on the ground, He prayed,

"Father, if You are willing, please take away this cup of horror from Me."
Luke 22:42 - The Living Bible

Jesus used the word "cup" to refer to that portion of His life. He was telling His Father that He didn't want to go through with the crucifixion if there could be another way to accomplish His Father's purpose.

Now, there is nothing wrong with desiring to quit. When the going gets extremely difficult, every athlete has that desire. Your natural tendency is to quit. How you handle that desire determines whether you are a winner from God's viewpoint. Let's see how Jesus handled His agony.

In the garden, He told His Father,

"But I want Your will, not mine."
Luke 22:42 - The Living Bible

Not only do we have the command (Colossians 3:17, 23) to give a total release in our union with Jesus Christ, but we also have His perfect example in the Garden of Gethsemane. Jesus totally released Himself to do His Father's will even when it meant He would experience great pain, death, and separation from His Father!

Only a few hours later, a Roman soldier, holding the feared scourge, awaited Jesus.

Scourging by Roman soldiers was done one of two ways, and in both, someone would strip the prisoner to the waist. Then the prisoner would either be bent over and tied to a stake, or he would be placed on the ground face down, arms and legs spread. Whichever method was used, the tormenting result was the same.

The soldier doing the scourging had a whip of three or more thongs. A sharp stone, piece of metal, or jagged bone was fastened at the end of each thong. Sometimes pieces of lead would also be fastened to the thongs, giving them additional weight for greater impact.

The person doing the scourging hit the victim at the base of his neck and quickly pulled the thongs, with the sharp implements embedded in the flesh, down the length of his back. One medical person researched the scourging of a cadaver—body of a dead person. He said that between the 18th and 25th lashing, the victim's skin was stripped from his back. A few more lashes would cut His flesh so badly you could push the flesh apart and see portions of his internal organs.

Once again, we see the winning character of Jesus as He totally released Himself toward His Father's purpose and relied on Him in this terrible situation to carry out that purpose.

Although Jesus had the desire to quit, He completely yielded Himself to His Father and His purpose for Him rather than give in to His own desires. Jesus proved Himself to be a winner through the Garden of Gethsemane ordeal and the painful Roman scourge. Yet, there was still a greater test to reveal His character. It took place on a hill outside Jerusalem.

One historian said that crucifixion was the most cruel way of putting a person to death. There were two main ways to crucify someone, each producing the same excruciating pain.

In the first, the person would be staked or tied to the cross that was flat on the ground. The cross and his body would then be lifted and plunged into a hole. In the second, the vertical beam would already be planted in the ground. The individual would be staked or tied to the horizontal beam, which would then be lifted and dropped into a slot on the vertical beam. The Bible indicates that Jesus was staked to the cross, causing Him to experience more pain than if He had only been tied.

In both methods of crucifixion, the victim's shoulders dislocated when the cross dropped into place, stopping abruptly. Then, with dislocated shoulders, the victim could not pull the weight of his body up to relieve pressure on his lungs, so breathing became difficult.

In fact, the only way that the victim could adequately breathe was to push his torso upward, trying to straighten his legs. However, because the flats of his feet were on the vertical beam, he could maintain this "breathing" position for only a few seconds. Then, because of the awkwardness of the position, he would collapse until he began gasping for air again. A malfunctioning nervous system would cause convulsions to wrack his body.

The Romans could keep a person alive for days, making crucifixion one of the most torturous ways of putting anyone to death.

Interestingly, Jesus could have kept Himself from this torturous death by denying that He was God. Most likely, His prosecutors would have dropped their charge against Him, and the crucifixion would not have occurred. At any point, Jesus could have quit. Instead, He totally released Himself toward His Father's purpose for Him in this situation.

At 3 p.m., what Jesus had feared in the Garden of Gethsemane happened. Separation from His Father in payment for our sins. At that moment, He cried out,

"My God, My God, why have You forsaken Me?"
Matthew 27:46 - The Living Bible

God the Father had totally separated Himself from His Son. Why? At that moment, Jesus paid the penalty for every wrong you and I have ever committed against God! Jesus totally gave Himself for you and me. He could have turned back from His mission, but He didn't. He was a winner by accomplishing His purpose for going to the cross.

In union with Jesus, by yielding to God to form Christ's attitudes, thoughts, and actions in and through you, you will never look on a defeat from an opponent as a loss.

1. *Read Luke 24:13-35. What stands out to you from this story?*
2. *Read 1 Peter 1:3, 8. What stands out to you from these verses about the impact of the resurrection on our lives?*
3. *The message of the Christian gospel that in Christ who died and rose again there is life. The hymn writer said, "Death cannot keep its prey, Jesus my Savior, He tore the bars away. Jesus my Lord, up from the grave He arose with a mighty triumph o'er His foes. He arose a victor from the dark domain, and He lives forever with His saints to reign. He arose, He arose, Hallelujah, Christ arose."*
4. *How do you respond to the resurrection?*

GOD USES EACH SITUATION

Remember, when Jesus hung dead on the cross, it looked as though He had been defeated...that He was a loser. Yet, this "defeat" was the setting for the greatest event in all history. On the third day, Jesus defeated death when He rose back to life. His resurrection demonstrated His power that is available in all your situations.

DON'T COMPARE PERFORMANCES

Athletes tend to compare their present performance with those of the past or expectations of the future. Your responsibility is to give what you do have, not what you don't have. Let's say as a quarterback you previously completed 19 out of 21 passes. The next time you complete only 6 out of 30 passes. Did you let down?

Perhaps, but not necessarily. Statistics depend on game conditions, quality of opponent, etc. God's perspective on winning depends only on to what degree you are focusing on Jesus and allowing God to conform you to the likeness of Jesus in your attitudes, thoughts, and actions.

You will never be sidetracked by the score, your opponent, or any other factor if you have a total release focus on Jesus and allow the Creator of the universe—who resides in you—to conform your attitudes, thoughts, and actions to Jesus. As you perform in this manner, you can know with confidence that the results of the competition will be His for whatever purpose He has in mind.

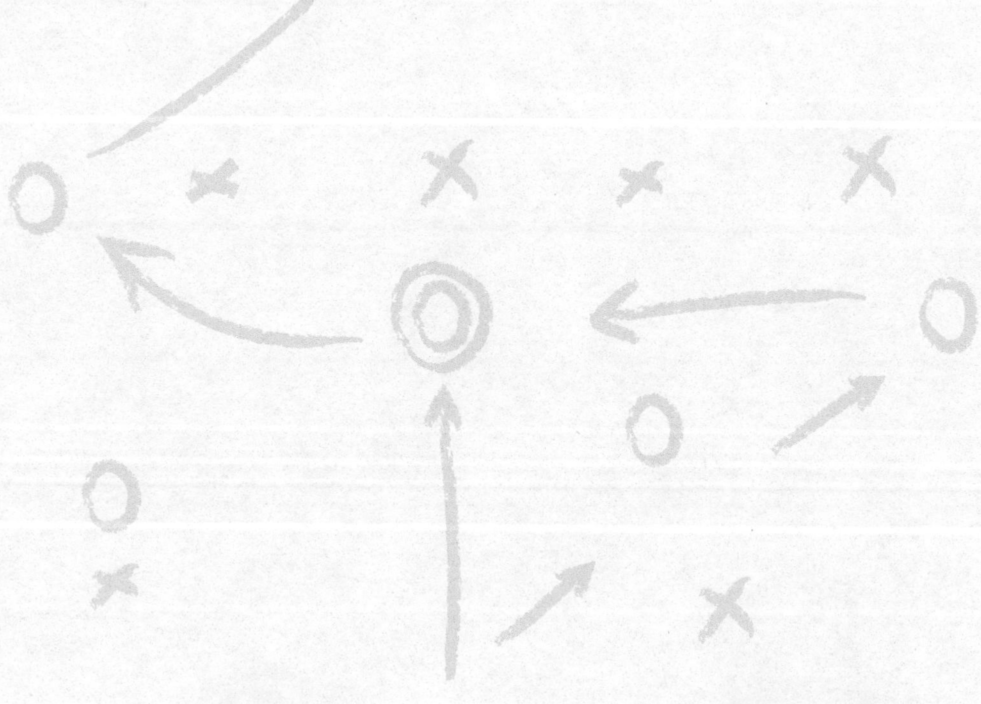

SCAN FOR
KINGDOM SPORTS MINUTE

SCAN FOR
CHAPTER LECTURES

CHAPTER EIGHT

JESUS IN PREPARATION

How would Jesus prepare for athletic competition? Perhaps this question is not as far-fetched as one might at first suspect it is.

The world of athletics is a microcosm of life itself. In one hour of athletic competition, an athlete can experience the same excitement, worry, frustration, fear, elation, depression, etc., that it would normally take a week or two to experience.

Since we can learn a lot about how we handle life by how we handle athletic situations, the opposite would equally hold true. We should be able to study how a person handles various life situations to determine how that person would handle different athletic situations.

So, by deduction, looking at how Jesus lived His life, we can determine how He would handle different athletic situations. In this chapter, our focus will be on how Jesus would prepare for athletic training sessions, practices, and competitions.

As we look at the everyday life of Jesus, we can observe at least three steps He would take in preparing to perform His Father's way.

STEP ONE

JESUS WOULD MAKE SURE HE WAS IN HARMONY WITH THE HOLY SPIRIT!

A Christ-Follower struggles with yielding to the Holy Spirit more in the athletic arena than in most nonathletic arenas. Why is that?

In athletics, there are so many distractions—both inwardly and outwardly—including people whose sole purpose for that moment is to rattle and defeat you. Athletic competition is the epitome of a hostile environment. Fortunately, Jesus was familiar with hostile environments.

In the hostile environment in which Jesus walked the dirt roads of Palestine, He and the Holy Spirit were mentally and spiritually in harmony, with His mind fixed on His Father.

As Jesus put it:

> *"... the Son can do nothing of his own accord, but only what he sees the Father doing. For whatever the Father does, that the Son does likewise."*
>
> **John 5:19**

To understand Jesus' connection to the Holy Spirit and His total focus on the Father, let's look at two ways He operated while He was walking those dirt roads.

A. Jesus did NOT rely on His equality with God the Father and the Holy Spirit.

Here's how Paul described Jesus' mindset:

> *"Have this attitude in yourselves which was also in Christ Jesus, who, although He existed in the form of God, did not regard equality with God a thing to be grasped, but emptied himself* [laid aside the use of His privileges as God], ***taking the form of a bondservant*** [one who is in total subjection to the one above him in a line of authority], ***and being made in the likeness of men*** [had to rely on the same source of power as we do]." [The brackets are mine]
>
> **Philippians 2:5-7**

Interestingly, although Jesus was God (John 1:18), He did not rely on His nature as God to handle difficulties. He could have, but He didn't.

B. Jesus totally relied on the Holy Spirit.

Jesus hiked out to a wilderness area immediately after He was baptized. During His 40 days in this remote area, He was mentally and spiritually preparing for His mission on a hostile Earth.

Now, did Jesus just decide on His own to get away from everyone for a while to prepare in the wilderness? No, the Holy Spirit led Him into the desolate area.

> *"**Then Jesus was led up by the spirit** into the wilderness to be tempted by the devil."*
>
> **Matthew 4:1**

The words "led up" tell us it was not Jesus' independent decision to go to the wilderness area. The Holy Spirit led Him. The same Spirit who lives in you as a true Christian—or Christ-Follower.

As an athlete, you have mental and physical abilities in which you can put your confidence. Jesus did, too. But He chose to place His confidence in His Father and His Father's ways as the Holy Spirit led Him, moment by moment.

As an athlete preparing for training sessions, practices, and competitions, Jesus would take time to make sure He was totally yielded to the Holy Spirit and in harmony with Him as a weapon for His Father.

HUDDLE UP!

1. *Discuss how athletics are a microcosm of life.*
2. *What is the importance of mentally and spiritually preparing for each training session, practice, and competition?*
3. *What can you learn from the prayer life of Jesus to help you in your athletic performance?*
4. *What are some wrong attitudes you've had in athletics (e.g., fear of opponent, recognition for self, wrong goal), and how can you deal with those attitudes in prayer?*
5. *How does continuously being alert to God's purpose affect your athletics?*

STEP TWO

JESUS WOULD COMMUNICATE WITH HIS FATHER IN PRAYER

Jesus prayed to prepare Himself for every situation, not just when He was in crucifixion mode. Praying was an exciting time for Jesus because He knew how to pray, and He experienced results when He talked with His Father.

Three of Jesus' episodes point out the priority that prayer had for Jesus and would have today if He were preparing for a training session, practice, or competition. And, in you, as one of His followers yielded to Him, He will be.

EPISODE #1 INVOLVES HIS ROUTINE LIFE.

Jesus was hugely popular throughout the land. He could not walk down the street without being recognized.

"But the news about Him was spreading even farther,
and great multitudes were gathering to hear Him and
to be healed of their sicknesses..."
Luke 5:15

This sort of people-filled day was as routine for Jesus as training sessions are for you. It was the same day after day.

The sameness could easily have sidetracked Jesus from His purpose, which was to accomplish His Father's assignment for Him (John 17:4). So, how did He handle the sameness?

The next verse describes what Jesus routinely did to avoid being sidetracked.

"But He Himself would often slip away to the wilderness and pray."
Luke 5:16

Jesus "often" slipped away to pray in the wilderness. It was not something He did only when He faced extreme pressure; it was His regular practice.

Now, the "wilderness" refers to any place where Jesus could be alone, with no distractions. You can, of course, have effective silent prayer in the middle of a noisy basketball game. But, for the most effective prayer, it's good to get off where there are no distractions. Like Jesus did...and will do through you.

EPISODE #2 INVOLVES JESUS CHOOSING HIS APOSTLES FROM AMONG THE LARGE NUMBER OF PEOPLE FOLLOWING HIM.

Selecting His men was a momentous occasion. These were key men He would train to take His message throughout the world, so each decision had to be the right one. Luke describes how Jesus prepared for His choices.

"And it was at this time that He went off to the mountains to pray, and He spent the whole night in prayer to God. And when the day came, ***He called His disciples to Him, and chose twelve of them, whom He also named apostles...****"*
Luke 6:12-13

Can you imagine praying for an entire night? That's the time for sleep. Yet, Jesus was about to make a series of the most important decisions of His life.

As He went to His Father for direction, the Holy Spirit led Him to pray all night. Remember, according to Philippians 2:5-7, Jesus completely emptied Himself of the use of His privileges as God for His earthly mission.

Jesus was in direct communication with His Father through prayer. And, through Jesus-driven prayer, we can also be in direct communication with God.

Here's the thing. Jesus spent time in prolonged prayer before every great decision or event. Likewise, there will be situations in which you will need to spend a longer time than usual in prayer.

It might be you are thinking about trying out for a team but wonder if you have the time. Or you might need insight into working out a problem with a teammate. These situations don't happen every day. They didn't for Jesus either. But when such important moments came, Jesus prepared for them in prolonged prayer. Not always all night, but longer than usual.

EPISODE #3 INVOLVES JESUS PREPARING FOR THE CRUCIFIXION.

Jesus approached this crisis event in prayer after He entered the Garden of Gethsemane with His disciples.

"And when he came to the place, he said to them, 'Pray that you may not enter into temptation.' ***And he withdrew from them about a stone's throw, and knelt down and prayed,*** *saying, 'Father, if you are willing, remove this cup from me. Nevertheless, not my will, but yours, be done.' And there appeared to him an angel from heaven, strengthening him.* ***And being in agony he prayed more earnestly; and his sweat became like great drops of blood falling down to the ground."***
Luke 22:39-42

Jesus was totally open and honest with His Father when He prayed. Fellowship is at its best when there is that kind of open and honest communication.

Jesus asked His Father to spare Him the unbearable pain of being separated from each other. But He also admitted that, above all, He did want to carry out His assignment...His Father's way. Jesus was in complete fellowship with His Father all the time, 24/7.

As an athlete in union with Jesus, the Holy Spirit might stir your mind to talk with your Father about your attitude toward practices and the fears you have. Then the Holy Spirit might use your mind to wholeheartedly express your desire to do it your Father's way.

In Paul's letter to the Philippians, he had just finished writing about his pursuit of Jesus when he wrote:

***"Let us therefore, as many as are perfect** [mature in Christ]**, have this attitude; and if in anything you have a different attitude, God will reveal that also to you..."** [The bracket is mine.]*
Philippians 3:15

The Holy Spirit will point out to you those attitudes not pleasing to God. For instance, let's say your opponent is undefeated and is determined to remain that way. You know your only athletic goal should be to focus on Jesus, yielding to the Holy Spirit to live His life in and through you, but you can't get your mind off your opponent's ability. It comes down to your being afraid of your opponent because you don't want to get beat.

In prayer and in union with Jesus, admit your fear to God because you want the Holy Spirit to control your thoughts. Agree with Him that this fear is not from Him. Trust Him to change your attitude of fear.

One passage the Holy Spirit might recall is Jesus' statement in **Luke 12:4:**

*"And I say to you, my friends, **do not be afraid of those who kill the body, and after that have no more than they can do."***

Of course, you are not afraid that your opponent will literally kill you. But the point is clear. Jesus is talking about an extreme. Fear of people comes from our natural mind. It is not a result of the Spirit-controlled mind. God is not afraid of people, and an athlete controlled by the Holy Spirit is not afraid of people.

Now, this does not mean you will necessarily beat your opponent. It simply means because of your responding to the Holy Spirit's dealing with your wrong attitude, you will be free to compete without being mentally shackled by fear.

You can see how important it is to study God's Word in the Bible. It enables the Holy Spirit to recall God's thoughts in your mind. He won't recall what isn't in your mind.

Honesty with God involves disclosing what you're really thinking. For instance, are you afraid of facing a particular challenge? You might try to convince yourself you're not afraid, but what is your real attitude?

Of course, what you disclose to God won't be news to Him. It won't catch Him by surprise. Your disclosing simply brings it out in the open for you to better "hear" from Him about it.

Now, here are four questions for you to consider that can get you started in being honest with God about what you're thinking...and feeling:

1. *On a scale of 1-5, how important is it for you to receive favorable recognition in the upcoming competition? Give a reason for your rating.*
2. *What is your greatest desire in the competition...and why is it?*
3. *What do you fear the most regarding this competition?*
4. *What do you look forward to the most in the competition?*

As you honestly disclose your thoughts to God and rely on Him to deal with them, the Holy Spirit will align your thoughts with His. Most of the time, He will do this by recalling portions of His Word stored in your mind.

STEP THREE

JESUS WAS ALERT TO HIS PURPOSE

Jesus prepared Himself by being continuously alert to His purpose, which was to accomplish His Father's assignment for Him. That alertness kept Him from being sidetracked.

For instance, Jesus got up early one morning and left the house while His men were still sleeping. In semi-darkness, He hiked to a lonely place where He prayed.

After sunrise, people from the town knocked on the door of Jesus's disciples' sleeping quarters. They wanted Jesus to heal more people, as He had done the evening before.

Peter and the rest of the disciples went hunting for Jesus to bring Him back to heal the sick. Now, when they found Him and excitedly told Him about all the people who wanted to be healed, you would think Jesus would have hurried back as fast as He could, wouldn't you?

What a shock it must have been to His disciples when He said,

"Let us go somewhere else to the towns nearby, in order that I may preach there also; for that is what I came out for."
Mark 1:38

Jesus knew that healing the sick was good. But His purpose was not to set up a medical practice. His purpose was to accomplish His Father's will that day to tell more people about His Kingdom.

Jesus sized up each situation for how it would relate to accomplishing His Father's purpose. For example, as the time approached for His crucifixion, He was alert as to how the crucifixion would tie into His Father's purpose for Him. So, instead of shying away from this difficult event, He pressed forward to meet it.

He told His Father,

"Now My soul has become troubled; and what shall I say, 'Father, save Me from this hour?' But for this purpose, I came to this hour."
John 12:27

Your one athletic goal is to focus on Jesus and yield to the Holy Spirit to express in and through you Jesus' thoughts, attitudes, and actions. Every training session, practice, and competition is an opportunity for this to happen. Allowing Jesus to prepare through you will help you stay connected to your Father in each situation.

CHAPTER NINE

JESUS IN ACTION

It has been said that "nice guys finish last." Jesus Christ would never have made an athletic team if that's true. Yet, studying His life reveals characteristics necessary for maximum athletic performance.

In fact, Jesus' life reveals far more outstanding athletic characteristics than most champions possess. True, He never jumped center or maneuvered the fast break in basketball. He never plunged over from the two-yard line or made a devastating block in football. He never experienced the thrill of a home run or lifted 400 pounds overhead.

But the characteristics Jesus displayed in His lifetime would have developed His physical and mental abilities to the maximum.

We can say this confidently because of the attitudes that shaped His life. Attitudes result in action. And His attitudes flowed out of His total surrender to the Holy Spirit.

As a result of His union with the Spirit, He engaged in a quality of action that would have made coaches crave His services for their teams.

So, in this chapter, let's look at just four of Jesus Spirit-driven attitudes. They will be your attitudes, as well, as you focus on Jesus and yield to the Holy Spirit to express the life of Jesus in and through you during your training sessions, practices, and competitions.

JESUS HAD THE ATTITUDE OF INTENSITY

Jesus totally directed His thoughts and actions toward accomplishing His Father's purpose in every situation. ***"...I do not seek My own will, but the will of Him who sent Me."*** **John 5:30**

ONENESS WITH HIS FATHER

Jesus was in complete oneness with His Father in every thought and action. And He never lost sight of His purpose, no matter how tough the situation.

For example, one day, Jesus and His men came to a water well in Samaria (John 4:1-42). He was tired and hungry after walking for many hours, and He needed a break along with the rest of His men. While Jesus was waiting at the well, His disciples went into the nearby town to bring back food for all of them to eat.

While Jesus' men were gone, a woman from the town came to draw water from the well. Although Jesus was tired, instead of keeping to Himself, He initiated a conversation that led to in-depth interaction.

That isn't natural for someone so tired, is it? However, because of Jesus' attitude of intensity for His Father's purpose in every situation, Jesus didn't give in to His tiredness. That woman and many people in the town came into God's family.

When Jesus' men returned to the well, they were amazed that He didn't immediately eat the food they brought Him.

"He said to them, 'I have food to eat that you do not know about.' The disciples therefore were saying to one another, 'No one brought Him anything to eat, did he?' Jesus said to them, ***'My food is to do the will of Him who sent Me,*** *and to accomplish His work.'"*
John 4:32-34

It wasn't that Jesus no longer needed food. It's that He was so intent on His Father's purpose that He didn't feel hungry anymore.

Physical fatigue first begins in our mind. We often believe we are tired long before our body needs to rest. Yes, getting rest is important. Yet, because our mind can be so focused on our own pleasure instead of Jesus, we often think we need to rest when we really don't.

If Jesus were in athletic competition today, His Spirit-driven attitude of intensity would develop His endurance to the maximum.

That doesn't mean it didn't hurt when the skin was ripped off His back in the scourge. He felt the pain of the scourge just as He would feel the spikes driven through His wrists. But He endured the pain because of His intense desire to fulfill His Father's purpose.

GIVING WHAT HE HAS

Now, even when your attention is on Jesus, you can experience times when fatigue does get to you. In fact, there can be times when pain refuses to let you continue.

Well, Jesus also experienced those times, like when He fell under the load of carrying His cross. But Jesus always gave what He had to give, even when He fell to the ground in pain and fatigue.

Although you can never give what you don't have, you must give what you do have. And when your focus is on Jesus, you will often find that you have more to give than you think.

So, how would Jesus use His attitude of intensity in a sport such as golf, where pain and exhaustion are minimal? Intensity starts in your mind, not in your muscles. Intensity is a matter of focus; from that focus comes the needed actions. Sometimes, a hard hit, other times a soft touch.

In golf, Jesus would focus on His Father's purpose for each shot. His practice swing would be just as important as His final putt: It has the same intensity different strokes.

IN UNION WITH JESUS

In union with Jesus, you will desire to accomplish your Father's purpose for that moment...through Jesus' thoughts, attitudes, and actions.

Okay, but how far does Jesus' attitude of intensity in you go? Let's say you injure your leg, and the doctor says you must sit out for three weeks to avoid long-term damage.

Consequently, you would not be demonstrating Jesus' attitude of intensity in carrying out His Father's assignment by insisting on playing. You might even be a detriment to the team because of your inability to be at your best.

Jesus' attitude of intensity only produced actions that were accomplishing His Father's purpose. One day, people became angry with Jesus because He had claimed to be God. In their frenzied anger, they picked up rocks to throw at Him. However, Jesus, in union with the Holy Spirit and His Father, hid himself from His attackers.

Jesus' attitude of intensity to accomplish His Father's purpose was just as great when He hid Himself as it was when He later boldly set off for Jerusalem, knowing that He would be crucified, a death far worse than stoning.

So, what was the difference? Jesus hid from those who wanted to stone Him because death at that time would not have accomplished His Father's purpose. Jesus was always intent on His Father's purpose, regardless of the circumstances.

You will experience Jesus' attitude of intensity as you continually get to know Him better and better, focus on Him, and yield to the Holy Spirit to express His attitudes in and through you.

JESUS HAD THE ATTITUDE OF FLEXIBLE-RIGIDITY

Jesus was rigid, or holding firm, in concentrating His efforts to accomplish His Father's purpose. That never changed, no matter how difficult the situation. However, Jesus was flexible about what action He would take to accomplish His Father's purpose.

When Jesus began His trek to Jerusalem, where He knew He would be crucified, His purpose was to accomplish the will of His Father. His Father's will in Jerusalem was for Jesus to pay the sin penalty for us on the cross.

Jesus remained rigid or firm in pursuit of that purpose. However, He was willing to change His actions to accomplish it. In the following episode, we see an example of His flexible-rigidity.

> *"And it came about, when the days were approaching for His ascension, that He resolutely set His face to go to Jerusalem; and He sent messengers ahead of Him.* ***And they went, and entered a village of the Samaritans, to make arrangements for Him. And they did not receive Him,*** *because He was journeying with His face toward Jerusalem. And when His disciples James and John saw this, they said,* ***'Lord, do you want us to command fire to come down from heaven and consume them?' But He turned and rebuked them. And they went on to another village."***
>
> **Luke 9:51-56**

Jesus knew it was not His Father's purpose to kill the Samaritans with fire. So, instead of insisting on staying where He had originally planned, in flexibility Jesus went on to another village.

Those extra miles were tough on already tired bodies. But Jesus' intense attitude toward accomplishing His Father's purpose enabled Him to push onward. Although He was rigid on His purpose, He was flexible on how to achieve it.

CHANGE PLANS, NOT PURPOSE

In athletic competition, Jesus' same attitude of flexible-rigidity would dictate the changing of plans to accomplish His Father's purpose, which doesn't change. He would simply move on to accomplish that purpose another way.

Let's say that you arrive at the locker room mentally and physically ready to give your best in the game. Then you notice on the bulletin board you are not listed as one of the starters. Now, if you were not focusing on Jesus, you might be greatly disappointed. After all, you came to help your team, not to watch it.

However, if you were yielding to the Holy Spirit to express Jesus in and through you, you would realize you could accomplish God's purpose even if you were not in the starting lineup. You can do that on the bench as well as on the playing field.

Or let's say that during a practice session, you're just standing around, not taking part in the action. Some of your teammates standing with you are joking among themselves.

However, in union with Jesus, His attitude of flexible-rigidity drives you to learn all you can as you watch the action. So, at the right time, you will be able to transfer your mental knowledge into physical action.

For example, in watching batting practice, you might be trying to learn something from the batter that you can apply to your swing.

That's Jesus' attitude of flexible-rigidity.

1. *What is the attitude of intensity, and how does it relate to your athletic performance?*
2. *Discuss when it is no longer wise to keep going. In other words, when is it right to stop or remove yourself from the contest?*
3. *How does the attitude of intensity relate to someone riding the bench or standing around during practices?*
4. *What is the attitude of flexible-rigidity, and how does it relate to your athletic performance?*

JESUS HAD THE ATTITUDE OF DIVINE-PERSPECTIVE

Divine-perspective is seeing people and situations through God's eyes.

This attitude kept Jesus from dwelling on the odds against Him. Now, odds are always human calculations. There is no such thing as odds in divine-perspective. To help grasp this truth, let's observe Jesus as He handled the death of one of His friends.

Jesus had received word that his friend, Lazarus, was very sick. In fact, Lazarus' two sisters hoped that Jesus would come immediately, trusting He could heal their brother. But Jesus didn't go. Now, that isn't the right way for a good friend to respond, is it?

Actually, it is the right way if that good friend is seeing the situation with divine-perspective. Jesus' purpose was to accomplish what His Father wanted. To do this, Lazarus would have to die.

Two days after Lazarus died, Jesus told His disciples they were all going to Bethany, where Lazarus and his sisters lived. His disciples were frightened because Bethany was close to Jerusalem. And it was in Jerusalem where religious leaders were plotting to kill Jesus.

From their natural perspective, Jesus' disciples wanted no part of that. They didn't want to go. But Jesus saw the death of Lazarus from His Father's perspective.

DIVINE-PERSPECTIVE WITH NO ODDS

Jesus and His men walked to Bethany, and Jesus talked with the two grieving sisters. Lazarus had already died. In fact, by the time Jesus and His men arrived, Lazarus had been in the tomb for four days.

There was no chance of Lazarus coming back to life. The odds were against it. But let's remember, odds are human calculations. They have nothing to do with how God sees it. With that in mind, let's capture the setting as John wrote about it.

> *"Then Jesus, deeply moved again, came to the tomb. It was a cave, and a stone lay against it. Jesus said, 'Take away the stone.' Martha, the sister of the dead man, said to him, 'Lord, by this time there will be an odor, for he has been dead four days.'* ***Jesus said to her, 'Did I not tell you that if you believed you would see the glory of God?'"***
>
> **John 11:38-40**

Here, we see what was in Jesus' mind throughout the entire ordeal. He was intensely moving toward accomplishing His Father's purpose through the death of Lazarus. Now, let's see how Jesus defied the human odds.

> *"So they took away the stone. And Jesus lifted up his eyes and said, 'Father, I thank you that you have heard me. I knew you always hear me, but I said this on account of the people standing around, that they may believe that you sent me.' When he had said these things,* ***he cried out with a loud voice, 'Lazarus, come out.' The man who had died came out, his hands and feet bound with linen strips, and his face wrapped with a cloth. Jesus said to them, 'Unbind him, and let him go.'"***
>
> **John 11:41-44**

A man who has been dead for four days is not supposed to come back to life. The human odds are just too great against something like that happening. It's physically "impossible."

But a Christ-Follower having the attitude of divine-perspective does not see the human odds or the impossibility of it. A Jesus-focused person sees every situation as an opportunity to totally rely upon God to accomplish His purpose.

That same attitude of divine-perspective would be with Jesus today in athletic competition. He would not be down if He is behind in the score. He would not give up hope if He were facing an undefeated opponent heavily favored to defeat Him.

WHEN GOD'S GLORY SHINES THE GREATEST

It is through a seemingly apparent defeat that God's greatest glory shines. Lazarus' death paved the way for his restored life. The crucifixion of Jesus preceded the great victory of His resurrection.

Circumstances did not shake Jesus' confidence in His Father. They simply provided opportunities for His Father's purpose to be achieved. Remember, "If God is for us, who is against us" (Romans 8:31).

With Jesus' divine-perspective, your purpose in each athletic situation is to accomplish your Father's assignment for you—one moment at a time.

JESUS HAD THE ATTITUDE OF CONTROLLED-EMOTION

Would Jesus lose His temper in athletic competition? Some people believe He would, based on how He chased the "rip-off artists" out of the temple.

However, as we carefully look at that temple cleansing episode, we'll see two things: 1) Jesus did not lose His temper, and 2) He used controlled-emotion to flavor His actions.

Actually, Jesus chased people out of the temple twice. He began His ministry that way (John 2:14-22) and ended it that way (Mark 11:11-18). Both times, He used controlled-emotion to flavor His actions.

Jesus had been in the temple many times before either of these episodes. He knew what was happening there. In the second episode, Jesus walked into the temple, looked around, and then returned to Bethany, where He was staying.

In Bethany, Jesus had a whole night to think over what He would do. He didn't return to the scene unemotional. Filled with emotion, Jesus was intent on achieving His Father's assignment to rid the temple of unethical profiteers.

FLAVOR IN ACTIONS

There was flavor in His actions. He didn't simply approach the sellers and coldly say, "Pardon me, but I believe you're trying to make a profit in My Father's house. That's not right. Now, please pick up your things and move on to the real marketplace."

Do you think the greedy bunch would have obliged Jesus? No! And Jesus knew that. He also knew exactly what actions were needed to clean up His Father's house. He rushed up to the tables and turned them over.

The first time, He used a scourge to chase out the animals. The second time, He drove the buyers and sellers out with His hands. The first time, He scattered the sheep and oxen. The second time, He would not even permit people to carry containers through the temple.

Jesus was a man of action. But He was also in complete control of what He was doing. In competitive sports today, Jesus would have His same attitude of controlled-emotion.

So, how can that affect your athletic performance?

Well, let's say, as a hockey player, someone has purposely tripped you. What's your first natural reaction? You want to retaliate and get even, don't you? You want revenge. Of course, taking revenge could give you momentary satisfaction. But let's see what else could happen:

1) Revenge could put you in the penalty box, and you would then be of no value to your team during that time; 2) You could inflict serious injury on the other player and, possibly, yourself; 3) You would fall short of your goal of focusing on Jesus and yielding to the Holy Spirit to express Jesus in and through you.

So, let's consider how you could handle the same situation with Jesus' attitude of controlled-emotion. The player purposely tripped you, and your first natural reaction might still be the urge to throw a punch in retaliation.

However, because you desire to have the attitude of Jesus, the Holy Spirit can recall to your mind these words in the Bible: "Never take your own revenge, beloved, but leave room for the wrath of God, for it is written, 'Vengeance is Mine, I will repay, says the Lord'" (Romans 12:19).

EMOTIONS WORKING FOR YOU

Retaliation is God's business, not yours. Your only goal is to focus on Jesus and yield to His Spirit in you. So, in union with Jesus, you agree with God that your initial idea of revenge is wrong.

Although the initial emotion is still in your emotional tank, you continue to skate, keeping your focus on Jesus. His controlled-emotion in and through you can give your actions more precision.

Instead of your natural emotion working against you, the Holy Spirit has channeled it to add greater emphasis to your actions as you surrender your mind to His control.

1. What is the attitude of divine-perspective, and how does it relate to your athletic performance?

2. What is the attitude of controlled-emotion, and how does it relate to your athletic performance?

3. What has been the result of you losing your temper?

4. When, if ever, is it right to lose your temper?

Jesus' thoughts, attitudes, and actions will maximize your athletic ability for what God has designed you. That development is an outflow of the Holy Spirit, conforming you to the likeness of Jesus Christ in your athletic performance.

SCAN FOR
KINGDOM SPORTS MINUTE

SCAN FOR
CHAPTER LECTURES

CHAPTER TEN

THE PERFECT MOTIVATION

One afternoon, a major league baseball player, Dave Roberts, stopped by the stadium gate to sign in his brother, Dan, to watch the game. However, when Dave reached for the clipboard that was supposed to be hanging from the bulletin board, he noticed it had fallen to the ground.

Apparently, another player had pulled it loose from the nail, used it, and then dropped it to the ground instead of putting it back up on the nail. Dave stooped down, picked up the clipboard, signed in his brother, and then paused for a moment. His natural inclination was to drop the clipboard back to the ground like everyone else had been doing. After all, it wasn't his problem.

Instead, Dave rearranged the things in his hands and fastened the clipboard to the nail again. Then, with a chuckle, Dave turned to Dan and remarked, "You know, doing what Jesus would do is the right thing, but it sure can be inconvenient."

INCONVENIENT IN PERFORMANCES, TOO

Dave was right, wasn't he? It can be inconvenient to think and do things Jesus' way. In fact, His way often conflicts with what we normally think and do.

Many times, we know what Jesus would want to do through us. But we don't yield to the Holy Spirit to express Jesus in and through us.

For example, we know that Jesus always fully gave Himself to whatever His Father wanted Him to do. So, it makes sense that He would want to fully give Himself in our athletics, too. But, because of our own desire—independent of Jesus—we don't always focus on Him or yield to Him to do that.

In this chapter, we are going to look at a biblical motivation that can keep you pursuing your goal of focusing on Jesus in each athletic situation and giving the mental green light to the Holy Spirit's activity, even when it's inconvenient…like when you don't feel like it.

SHORTCOMINGS OF NATURAL MOTIVATIONS

Before we check out that motivation, let's consider two shortcomings of natural athletic motivations: anger, revenge, personal recognition, etc. Motivations that are naturally part of us.

SHORTCOMING # 1

First, these motivations can never help you consistently perform at your best. Why? Because each must have the right circumstances to make them work. And you won't always have the right circumstances.

For example, revenge can't work when you don't want to get even with someone. Anger can't work if you don't have a reason to be angry. And your desire for recognition isn't going to help you perform any better if people aren't aware of how good you are...or don't care.

SHORTCOMING # 2

Second, the biggest problem with natural motivations is they are not Christlike. For example, Jesus did not seek revenge on those who opposed Him. He did not get angry even when people spit on Him and ripped the skin off His back in the feared Roman scourge. And Jesus only sought recognition for His Father, not Himself.

Those natural motivations didn't drive Jesus when He walked the roads of Palestine, and they won't drive Him when you yield to the Holy Spirit to live His life in and through you today.

So, using natural motivations, you won't experience athletic perfection—doing sports God's way. But there is one motivation that did and does drive Jesus. And it's a powerful one.

MOTIVATION OF GOD'S LOVE

Interestingly, God the Father's love for Jesus is the same love He has for you. And Jesus' love for His Father is the same love He has for you as one of His followers. Jesus expressed that love—for His Father and you—in everything He said and did.

However, one event more graphically displays it. So, let's take a moment to look at that one event...His crucifixion. Again, Jesus' expression of His love for you on the cross is the Father's love for you—*"For God so loved the world that He gave His only Son..."* (John 3:16).

SWEATING IN THE COOL EVENING

Jesus led His disciples to the Garden of Gethsemane, just across a ravine from Jerusalem. Although it was in the cool of the evening, Jesus was in so much mental and emotional turmoil that He was sweating. He was sweating so profusely that "His sweat became like drops of blood, falling down upon the ground" (Luke 22:44).

Luke, a medical doctor, is the only one of Jesus' four biographers that mentions this important fact. It has been medically established that blood vessels close to the skin's surface can burst if a person is under enough emotional strain. The blood could then ooze through the skin, making a bloody sweat.

Although it was possible, because of Jesus' severe emotional strain, that blood did appear on His face, Luke didn't say that Jesus did sweat blood. He said that Jesus' sweat became "like" drops of blood falling to the ground.

Whether it was real blood or a thick and heavy sweat, it was unusual for a person to sweat in the cool of the evening. In either case, tremendous emotional strain was wracking Jesus' mind and body.

COMMITMENT TO HIS FATHER

Then, in prayer, Jesus committed Himself to do what His Father wanted Him to do—"not my will, but your will be done"—to go to the cross in our place. So, in an amazing act of love for His Father and for us, Jesus willingly gave Himself over to the soldiers who had been sent out to capture Him.

The soldiers took Jesus back to Jerusalem, where one "witness" after another made false accusations against Him. Yet, through it all, Jesus did not defend Himself. He remained silent, bent on carrying out His Father's will.

Finally, Roman soldiers ripped the skin off His back with the Roman scourge, pounded a crown of spike-like thorns onto his head, and beat His face with the palms of their hands.

Think about it! The Romans treated Jesus like a common criminal. They had no idea that the God who created this entire universe and gave them His breath of life was allowing them to treat Him how they might treat a sadistic killer.

Jesus allowed Himself to be physically tortured in carrying out His Father's assignment of love and paying our death penalty for us. But it didn't end there. That was only the start. The worst was yet to come.

The soldiers led Jesus outside of Jerusalem to a place where they nailed Him to the cross by hammering heavy spikes through His wrists and feet. Some soldiers then raised Him on the cross to an upright position and let the cross slam to the bottom of a hole with a thud.

The abrupt stop would have jarred Jesus' shoulders to a painful dislocation. And His torso would have slumped forward, pulling against His torn and dislocated shoulders.

In this sagging position, Jesus would feel a tremendous squeeze on His lungs, making breathing difficult. In trying to take in some air, He would push up with His legs, but because the flat of His feet were nailed to the upright beam of the cross, He would not be able to straighten His legs.

In that awkward position, after a short and shallow gulp of air, He would slump once again. This repeated movement up and down on the cross would make any victim look like an extremely slow human yo-yo.

MOST CRUEL PUNISHMENT

Medical doctors tell us that the spikes through his wrists most likely would have severed nerves, which would have sent shock waves throughout his body, with a gnawing pain. Before long, His malfunctioning nervous system would have given His body a significant temperature rise, only to be followed by severe chills.

The great Roman orator Cicero regarded crucifixion as "a most cruel and disgusting punishment." Some victims survived several days on the cross, only to die stark-raving mad.

Jesus' agonizing death on the cross was His expression of love for His Father. And it was also the most logical and reasonable way for Him to shout out His love for us—our Father's love for us.

PAUL'S ROMANS 12:1 CHARGE

The apostle Paul wrote:

> ***"I urge you, therefore, brethren, by the mercies of God*** *[because of how God demonstrated His love for you on the cross],* ***to present your bodies*** *[consciously commit your physical abilities to God],* ***a living and holy sacrifice*** *[dead to your own interests and alive to God's interests]* ***acceptable to God, which is your spiritual service of worship*** *[the most logical way for you to express your love and reverence to God]."*
>
> **Romans 12:1** [The added brackets are mine.]

In this passage of instruction, Paul directs the thoughts of his readers to use all their physical talents for God's purpose. Although Paul was not writing with the athlete in mind, your athletic abilities are included in the word he used for "bodies."

It's a Greek word that refers to all one's physical characteristics, both seen and unseen, including one's athletic abilities (e.g., reflexes, speed, strength, coordination, etc.). So, God wants you, as an athlete, to present to Him the use of all your athletic abilities.

Here's the point. Because of what God did for us—Jesus' suffering on the cross in paying our sin-penalty—He desires us as Christ-Followers to express our love for Him with everything we have.

FACTS ABOUT ROMANS 12:1

Let's consider four more points about this Romans 12:1 passage to get a clear understanding of how God wants us, in union with Jesus, to be motivated.

1. The verb *"present"* means to turn over to someone the control of something you have. For example, if you "present" a baseball glove to someone, you have given that person the right to use your glove. In this passage, Paul instructs us to present, or turn over the control of, our bodies to God for His use of them.

2. The phrase *"a living and holy sacrifice, acceptable to God,"* describes the quality of what you give to God. The words "living and holy" tell us that what you give Him is for His use. In other words, God can use whatever you present to Him in any way He chooses.

   The word *"sacrifice"* means that you're totally giving up what you present. It is no longer for your own use. A sacrifice has no claim on anything.

   Now, here's the thing. Only Christlike thoughts, attitudes, and actions are acceptable to God. So, athletically speaking, you are to use your abilities exactly as Jesus Christ himself would and will use them...as you yield to the Holy Spirit to flesh out Jesus through you.

3. The phrase *"spiritual service of worship"* describes any activity that is an expression of your love and respect for God. Applied to athletics, this phrase opens a new and exciting way for you to approach your workouts and competitions.

   The phrase could also be stated, "The logical and reasonable way for you to express your love and respect for God." Since you are an athlete, this "logical and reasonable way" includes your athletic performance.

4. Paul's first phrase in Romans 12:1, *"by the mercies of God,"* tells why you should even want to use your athletics to express your love and respect for God. The word "mercy" means "compassion."

   The phrase literally means, "because of the compassion God has shown you." Most notably, it can refer to God's loving compassion that Jesus demonstrated on the cross by paying your sin-penalty.

As a Christian athlete, you can express your love for Jesus for what He has done for you in each training session, practice, and competition. How? By focusing on Him and yielding to the Holy Spirit to live the thoughts, attitudes, and actions of Jesus in and through you.

LIKE FLOWING THROUGH A NOZZLE

Paul wrote, *"For the love of Christ controls us..."* **2 Corinthians 5:14**

The Greek word for "controls" describes what a nozzle on the end of a hose does to the water coming through the hose. It thrusts the normal flowing water forward with an intensified force. Paul was saying that Jesus' love for His Father and for him channeled all of Paul's actions in an expression of love for Jesus.

1. ***How does the baseball player signing in his brother to watch a game illustrate a common problem that Christian athletes have? In what way might it be a problem for you...if it is?***
2. ***What are some of your natural motivations, and how has each affected your athletic performance?***
3. ***What are two shortcomings of most natural motivations?***
4. ***Considering Jesus' crucifixion, how can being aware of God's love for you be more powerful than most natural motivations?***
5. ***Using Romans 12:1, how can the quality of your athletic performance reveal the quality of your love for God?***

AN OLD TESTAMENT EXAMPLE

In the Old Testament, we have a good example of an action motivated by love. Three of King David's top warriors risked their lives to get him a drink of water from his hometown well. Here's how it played out.

'And three of the thirty chief men went down and came about harvest time to David at the cave of Adullam when a band of Philistines was encamped in the Valley of Rephaim.

"David was then in the stronghold, and the garrison of the Philistines was then at Bethlehem. And David said longingly, 'Oh, that someone would give me water to drink from the well of Bethlehem that is by the gate!'

"Then the three mighty men broke through the camp of the Philistines and drew water out of the well of Bethlehem that was by the gate and carried and brought it to David."
2 Samuel 23:13-16a

THREE FRIENDS' EXPRESSION OF LOVE

Three men risked their lives to get David a drink of water. You'd think he was dying of thirst. Keep in mind that David was a veteran of roaming the hills and leading an army of men. Such a leader would not bring his men to a campsite without plenty of drinking water. David and his men had water.

When David's three friends first arrived for their visit, they spent some time talking with David. Apparently, during this conversation, David reminisced about the cool and good-tasting water from his hometown well in Bethlehem. He expressed a craving for it out of sentiment and taste, but he never commanded his friends to get any for him. He wouldn't think of doing that.

David's three friends left him at the cave, broke through enemy lines, maneuvered their way to the well, and drew a pitcher of water. Their lives were endangered with every step they took. In fact, they were probably a battle-worn threesome when they arrived back at David's cave.

All this for a pitcher of water? It doesn't make sense, does it? But how about what David did then?

DAVID'S EXPRESSION OF LOVE

"But he would not drink of it. He poured it out to the LORD and said,
"Far be it from me, O LORD, that I should do this. Shall I drink
the blood of the men who went at the risk of their lives?" Therefore
he would not drink it. These things the three mighty men did."
2 Samuel 23:16b-17

David knew his friends didn't risk their lives for a pitcher of water. They risked their lives for him. David knew it was their way of saying, "We love you." Most likely, David had been their leader since they joined the army. Perhaps that's all he was at first. But after going through many battles together, David became their friend. He cared for them, wept with them, and laughed with them.

Over time and many shared adventures, their respect for David as a leader developed into a love for him as a man. It developed to the point where these three great friends were willing to risk death as an expression of their love for him. Intense love toward someone can reproduce itself in intense action for that person.

GO DEEP

1. *Why did David do what he did when his friends brought him a pitcher of water?*
2. *How can you apply what David did to each of your training sessions, practices, and competitions?*
3. *How has using your athletics, in union with Jesus, be an expression of your love for God, or how would you like it to be?*

BRINGING IT HOME

Love for God is the only perfect motivation. It's also Jesus' only motivation as you yield to the Holy Spirit to express Him in and through you in your training sessions, practices, and competitions.

As you read the following account of what happened to a college track athlete, as one of Jesus' followers...who happens to be an athlete...be thinking of internalizing the content of this chapter. This account is from a letter the athlete sent me:

"In four years of cross-country and track in high school, I never qualified for the state meet. My failure caused me to think negatively about my abilities, and I felt sorry for myself for having to endure so much pain in the workouts.

"My negative thinking continued into college. Even after I accepted Christ in my life, I still had negative thoughts about my future in athletics.

"In the conference meet, because I wasn't feeling well, I asked a friend to pray for me. He promised to pray, but he also gave me a sports booklet describing what Jesus went through on the cross for me.

"Reading about Jesus' crucifixion made me want to run the race just to show my love for Him, not to win the trophy. That was the first time I ever won a conference meet. And I was even sick.

"With my new awareness of God's love for me and my desire to use my running to express my love back to Him, I even went on to win the state championship."

Love for God is the only perfect motivation. It's also Jesus' only motivation as you yield to the Holy Spirit to express Him in and through you in your training sessions, practices, and competitions.

SCAN FOR
KINGDOM SPORTS MINUTE

SCAN FOR
CHAPTER LECTURES

CHAPTER ELEVEN

OVERCOMING NEGATIVES

A negative force in athletics is anything that has the potential to negatively affect your performance. It can be fear, injury, fatigue, pain, anger, a preoccupied mind, etc. You can even think of your opponent as a negative force.

Obviously, it's important to overcome negative forces. In fact, how successful you are in overcoming the negatives will determine to what degree you experience athletic perfection—doing it God's way.

In this chapter, we'll cover how to overcome negative forces through the motivation of the love we covered in the last chapter.

However, before we do that, let's look at four hypothetical examples of different negative forces just to have a mental picture of the devastation they can cause.

EXAMPLE ONE

Brad, an offensive lineman in football, is dealing with the two negative forces of anger and resentment. The team's main running back has publicly been glorying in his long runs as if he were making them by himself. He never gives credit to his line for opening the holes.

Brad knows that if he and the other linemen were not opening the holes, the running back would not gain more than two yards a carry. The running back's "me-me" attitude has begun to affect Brad's intensity whenever the running back is involved. Consequently, Brad's anger and resentment are hurting the team.

EXAMPLE TWO

The success of Anne's basketball team revolves around her aggressive rebounding. Five games ago, in going for a rebound just as the third quarter started, an elbow to her eye put her on the bench for the rest of the game. Lots of pain…and seven stitches were needed.

In Anne's next game, five days later, an elbow hit her in the mouth, loosening two teeth. Again, lots of pain.

Since that last elbow, Anne has been less aggressive on the boards, allowing her opponents to control both ends of the court, and her team has been suffering for it. Her own shooting has even dropped off.

EXAMPLE THREE

Pro golfer, Sarah, is tied for the lead toward the end of the final round in one of the three most important tournaments of the season.

As she is teeing her ball for the final hole of the tournament, she hears a thunderous roar of approval from the spectators around the 16th green. She assumes her co-leader had just made a great putt for a birdie and a one-stroke lead.

Sarah realizes she must get a birdie on a hole that has given her difficulty in the first three rounds—a lucky par followed by two bogeys. It just isn't a birdie-hole for her skill set. The negative force of her recent failures on the hole weighs heavily on her.

EXAMPLE FOUR

Sam knows it will take an all-out effort to defeat his opponent in the finals for the national wrestling championship. He has trained hard for the match, and he knows his opponent has, also.

The match begins at a furious pace, and for two periods, the athletes wrestle to a standoff. They seem to be equal in technique, speed, and strength. As they rest on their backs for a few seconds, awaiting the third period, Sam notices the big difference between them. His opponent is not breathing nearly as hard as he is. Sam is feeling the negative force of exhaustion.

Toward the end of the chapter, we will see how the athletes in these four hypothetical examples overcame the negative forces by applying the lessons we will now cover.

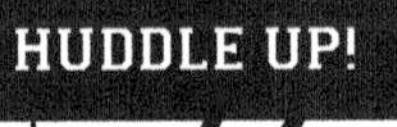

1. *Name some negative forces and explain how they can hinder your athletic performance.*
2. *With which of the four hypothetical examples do you most closely identify, and why?*
3. *What is the worst suffering you have faced as an athlete? What has God taught you through it?*

FOCUSING ON JESUS

Lamaze classes are taught throughout the country to prepare a woman for childbirth. The classes have helped thousands of women experience joy rather than pain and fear in birthing. These classes teach us an amazing truth about how the human brain works.

You would see a strange sight if you walked into a class where husbands and wives were taught the Lamaze method. You would see pregnant women slowly moving their fingers in circular motions over their abdomens while breathing slowly and controlled. You would also notice that these women were staring at a fixed point, usually an inanimate object in the room. Their husbands would be present to encourage and coach them.

FOCUS ON ONE THING AT A TIME

The premise of Lamaze is that the brain can focus or concentrate, at 100% capacity, on only one thing at a time. So, to block out the discomfort of labor, the woman tries to concentrate on three things simultaneously: 1) her focal point on the inanimate object, 2) her controlled breathing, and 3) her fingers making slow circular motions on her abdomen.

Pain must register in the brain, but a preoccupied brain is less aware of it, especially when the brain is trying to focus on three things, not just one.

Negative forces are part of every athletic contest. You cannot escape them. Some attack your mind. Others attack your body. They all try to stifle your performance.

Overcoming those negative forces is one of the great benefits that will be yours as you keep your focus on Jesus and, in union with the Spirit of Christ in you (Romans 8:9), express Jesus' love for the Father through your athletic performance. We might consider this focus on Jesus as the Lamaze method in athletic perfection.

HOW LOVE OVERCOMES NEGATIVE FORCES

In the last chapter, we touched on the athletic implications of **Romans 12:1**. This great passage is the key to understanding HOW love conquers negative forces. Paul wrote:

> ***"I urge you therefore, brethren, by the mercies of God, to present your bodies a living and holy sacrifice, acceptable to God, which is your spiritual service of worship."***

ROMANS 12:1 APPLIED TO ATHLETICS

Now, let's understand the passage as if Paul were writing just to you as a Christian athlete pursuing athletic perfection.

The word *"brethren"* tells us that Paul was writing to fellow Christians. His phrase, *"by the mercies of God,"* could also be rendered "because of what God accomplished for you by Christ dying on the cross." So, what follows is your response to what Christ did.

The verb *"present"* simply means to turn over to someone else the control of something you have, like your body. Because the word "body" refers to all your physical characteristics, it includes all your athletic abilities (e.g., your reflex action, speed, strength, coordination, etc.).

Paul's next phrase, *"living and holy sacrifice,"* is what makes it possible for you to overcome negative forces. It refers to you, dead to yourself (sacrifice), and alive to the Spirit of Christ in you. This reality in your athletic performance makes it *"acceptable"* to God for His purpose.

The last phrase, *"spiritual service of worship,"* can also be rendered "the logical way for you to express your love for God." With that in mind, let's camp on this last phrase for a moment.

The Greek word used for *"service of worship"* describes any form of service that results out of a love relationship with God. It includes your athletic performance, along with anything else that you do.

For example, two javelin throwers let the javelins fly with all their energy. The javelins sail through the air and land. God is pleased with one performance but not the other. Why? Motivation. It has nothing to do with how far each javelin goes. One athlete threw the javelin for his own personal glory. The other athlete threw the javelin as an expression of his love for God.

Keep in mind that the phrase "service of worship" includes running the bases as well as tackling a running back. It includes dribbling a basketball downcourt as well as blocking a volleyball spike or throwing a javelin. It includes everything you will ever do in your athletic performance. This "service" is a love expression to God.

YOUR LOGICAL EXPRESSION

If you were a shepherd in the Old Testament days, it would be logical for you to select the best lamb to give back to God as an expression of your love. Since you are an athlete rather than an Old Testament shepherd, it isn't logical for you to offer a lamb on the altar as an expression of your love for God.

However, it is logical for you to offer your athletic ability on the "altar" of the basketball or volleyball court, football or soccer field, baseball or softball diamond, wrestling mat, golf course, etc.

Your athletic abilities are a gift from God. Since you are an athlete, it is logical for you to offer the best quality of your abilities to Him as an expression of your love. That logical way to express your love for God is the "spiritual" way...and will overcome the negative forces you are dealing with.

AN ATHLETIC PARAPHRASE OF ROMANS 12:1

"I urge and encourage you, **(insert your name)**, because of what God accomplished for you when Jesus Christ died on the cross, to place all your athletic abilities at God's disposal throughout your athletic performance. Keep your focus on Jesus and allow the Holy Spirit to express the life of Jesus in and through your thoughts, attitudes, and actions. This not only will be acceptable to God, but it is the most logical way you can express your love to Him tangibly while you are training, practicing, and competing."

Tom's Experience

Here's an example of how Tom applied Romans 12:1 to his athletic performance. He explains his experience overcoming negative forces during one of the biggest wrestling tournaments of the year.

"Each year, there are between 35 and 50 wrestlers in a weight class, so you must win a lot of preliminary matches to reach the finals. I entered the tournament with a great desire to place. More importantly, I wanted to give a total release of all that I was in my union with Jesus.

"I barely won my first match on a ride time point that was given to me after the match ended in a tie. During the match, I wasn't doing as well as I had planned. All I could think of was, 'Oh no! Tom, you're going to mess up again in this big tournament.'

"At one point when I was behind, the thought raced through my mind that I might just as well give up since I wasn't wrestling as well as I could have. But I knew that wouldn't be a total release performance. I decided to wrestle to the best of my ability for the rest of the match and leave the outcome to God.

"I ended up winning, but I still knew something was keeping me from really experiencing the feeling of going all out physically, mentally, and spiritually. I just didn't know what it was.

"My next match was against a guy who had pinned me when we wrestled two years earlier. We wrestled about even for the first two periods, but I soon sensed that I wasn't free. Something was keeping me from following through with my moves. I ended up losing the match 7-3.

"I hoped that the guy who just beat me would continue to win his matches so that I would be able to wrestle in the consolation bracket. He did. That gave me a chance to come back again later that night.

"I was really confused because I wasn't performing up to my potential even though I had prepared for the match, and I wanted to express my love to Jesus through it.

"That night, I won my first consolation match by a decision and my second one by a forfeit.

"After thinking about it and praying later that night, I finally realized what my problem was. I had been trying to give a total release of myself to perform like Jesus, but I had taken my eyes off Him.

"I had been focusing my attention on the tournament and the other wrestlers in my weight class. I had been thinking about all the matches I would have to win to earn a place. As a result, I wasn't free in my mind to give a real total release of my potential.

"The next day was completely different. I kept my focus on Jesus instead of the number of matches and who my opponent would be. I committed each present match as a love expression to the Lord. I just took them one at a time. I was able to beat my next three opponents while, at the same time, I was experiencing the freedom to wrestle to my potential.

"In fact, my last match was against the same wrestler who had defeated me the night before. I won this match 5-3, even though it was only 24 hours later.

"I learned I had to do the same thing Jesus did when He went to the cross. He kept His eyes on His Father and on His Father's assignment for Him and simply went out to finish the task His Father called Him to do…as His love expression."

1. ***Explain how love overcomes negative forces in your union with Jesus, according to Romans 12:1.***
2. ***How does Romans 5:3-5 relate to setbacks?***
3. ***Read Proverbs 3:5-6. What does this passage teach you about athletics and life? Why is it difficult to trust God?***
4. ***According to Philippians 4:6-7, how can prayer help you overcome a difficult situation?***
5. ***What does it mean to "consider it all joy" in James 1:2? When you encounter problems, is joy a choice or an emotion?***

NEGATIVE FORCES DEFEATED

If the only desire of the athletes in our opening hypothetical examples was to express love for God through their athletic performance, how would they have handled their negative forces? Let's find out.

SOLUTION FOR EXAMPLE ONE

Brad is not concerned with getting credit for his performance since his only audience is God. He takes the truth of Colossians 3:23 seriously, where he is told to do his work heartily for the Lord rather than for other men.

Since Brad has committed his line play to be an expression of love for God, his attention is not diverted by the acclaim given to one of the running backs.

In fact, he feels satisfied knowing that he is doing what God has for him, and he is contributing to the team by helping make it possible for the running back to gain the yards.

SOLUTION FOR EXAMPLE TWO

Anne realizes that physical injury is the possible by-product of any physical activity. She decided to use each performance as an expression of love for God.

She couldn't tell much difference at first. Fear of the "sharp" elbows was still on her mind. It wasn't until Anne realized that what Jesus endured on the cross was His expression of love for His Father—and for her—that she kept her eyes on Jesus rather than on the fear of pain and injury.

Now, Anne mentally prepares for each practice and game by picturing herself going after rebounds as an expression of love for God. Because of her preparation, she looks forward to the challenge of clearing the boards.

SOLUTION FOR EXAMPLE THREE

It was relatively easy for Sarah to concentrate on each golf shot as a separate expression of love for God. She realized there was nothing she could do about someone else's score.

When Sarah understood that "God causes ALL things to work together for good to those who love God, to those who are called according to His purpose" (Romans 8:28), she was free to concentrate only on expressing love for God.

SOLUTION FOR EXAMPLE FOUR

Sam's "one arm tied behind his back" because of exhaustion was quickly untied when he set his attention back on Jesus and yielded to the Holy Spirit to use his performance as an expression of Christ's love for His Father.

He realized that if God desired him to defeat his opponent, God could give him the endurance no matter how tired he felt. His only responsibility was to unleash all he did have, in union with Jesus, as an expression of love.

GOD'S HALL OF FAME EXAMPLES

Charles Thomas (C.T.) Studd, was a British missionary to China, India, and Africa, as well as considered to be England's most outstanding cricket player. In the mission field, Studd understood from the Bible and his own daily experience how to handle the negative forces that continually came at him.

"If Jesus Christ be God and died for me," he said, "then no sacrifice can be too great to make for Him."

If Studd were speaking to you, he might add, "Including sacrifice in your athletic performance."

Of course, for Christians to sacrifice their natural desires because of their commitment to Jesus is really nothing new. Foxe's Book of Martyrs contains true stories of people who were willing to be tortured to death rather than deny their commitment to follow Jesus.

IGNATIUS

For example, Ignatius, the great bishop of Antioch, was scourged and practically skinned alive by people who tried to force him to deny his faith in Jesus. Then, they tied papers dipped in oil to his side and set the papers on fire while they also put fire in his hands.

To top it off, the torturers tore Ignatius' flesh with hot pincers and left him for wild animals to rip apart. Ignatius could have given into his natural desire to experience no pain and go on living. All he would have had to do was publicly deny his faith in Jesus. But Ignatius loved Jesus more than his own life and refused to publicly turn against His Lord…and closest friend.

MORE HEROES OF THE FAITH

Foxe tells of one man who was whipped, put into a leather bag with serpents and scorpions, and thrown into the sea to drown. Another man had fire put into his hands before he was hung by his feet while salt and vinegar were poured into his nostrils.

Still, another committed follower of Jesus had his body seared with hot irons. He was then put on the rack to be tortured. Afterward, hot coals were dumped on his freshly shaved head.

Christians down through the centuries have given us example after example of self-sacrifice in their expressions of love and respect for Jesus.

These men and women knew the fullest implications of Romans 12:1. By presenting their bodies to the Lord as a living sacrifice, they expressed their love to Him for what He had done for them on the cross. God used their deaths to encourage other Christians to keep on fighting the good fight.

IT'S ALWAYS A CHOICE

Sure, your training sessions, practices, and competitions are not nearly as torturous as what these Christian martyrs experienced. But your choice is just as real.

It's quite possible that God will never call you to make this kind of sacrifice. You might never have to choose between Jesus and your own physical life. But you do have a choice to make between Jesus and yourself every time you go through a drill or carry out an athletic assignment.

Your choice is between whether you focus on Jesus or yourself. It's between yielding to the Holy Spirit to express Jesus' love for the Father through your thoughts, attitudes, and actions or simply doing the drill or assignment as best you can on your own.

Your choice is between using your drills and assignments as expressions of love for God or yielding to the negative forces against you.

It's always a choice.

SCAN FOR
KINGDOM SPORTS MINUTE

SCAN FOR
CHAPTER LECTURES

CHAPTER TWELVE

THE PRAISE PERFORMANCE

The shortstop crouches, ready to spring into action. At the crack of the bat, he races to his left and quickly scoops the ball into his glove. While on the dead run, he twists his body, cocks his arm, and throws the runner out at first base. If his action had a voice, you would hear it cry, "Praise the Lord!"

In a split second, the basketball guard steals the ball and dribbles halfway down the court. Then, with pinpoint accuracy, she passes to a teammate who drives in for an easy lay-up. If their actions had voices, they would shout, "Praise the Lord!"

On the snap of the ball, the wide receiver begins his moves. With a hip fake and foot plant, he breaks to the right. The ball is in the air, spiraling for its target. The wide receiver and defender lunge for the ball at the same time. With his fingers extended beyond what he thought was possible, the receiver grabs the ball and falls to the turf. If his action could speak, it would be shouting, "Praise the Lord!"

PRAISE GOD WITH YOUR ATHLETIC ABILITIES

Can you actually do that? Is it possible to praise the Lord with your athletic performance? You will have an excitement for even the most routine drill when you understand the implication that Psalm 150 has for your athletic performance.

Yes, it is possible to praise the Lord through the different bodily motions of your athletic performance. One way to express your love for God is by sincerely praising Him. In fact, God has designed you to praise Him.

Because your voice is a gift from God, you can sing His praises. And, because your physical abilities are also gifts from God, with them, you can express your praise of Him.

In union with Jesus, what greater experience can you possibly have in your training sessions, practices, and competitions than to unleash your love for God by praising Him through your actions?

PSALM 150

The writer of Psalm 150 put it this way:

1) "Praise the Lord! Praise God in His sanctuary; Praise Him in His mighty expanse.

2) "Praise Him for His mighty deeds. Praise Him according to His excellent greatness.

3) "Praise Him with trumpet sound; Praise Him with harp and lyre.

4) Praise Him with timbrel and dancing; Praise Him with stringed instruments and pipe.

5) "Praise Him with loud cymbals. Praise Him with resounding cymbals.

6) Let everything that has breath praise the Lord. Praise the Lord."

WHAT PRAISE IS

What a tremendous psalm. It explains ***where*** to praise God (verse 1), ***why*** to praise Him (verse 2), and ***how*** to praise Him (verses 3-5). It also explains ***who*** should praise Him (verse 6).

So, let's define what the Bible means by praising God. The word "praise" first means "to shine." Then, it means "to make clear." Finally, it means "to exclaim in a loud tone."

Isn't that what Psalm 150:3-5 describes? Those verses describe a blend of musical instruments in one great symphony of sounds. Their purpose is to ***shine*** forth the greatness of God, to focus ***clearly*** on Him, and to shout out His praises in a ***loud*** tone. The purpose of the instruments is to praise the Lord!

WHERE AND WHY TO PRAISE GOD

Where are we to praise God? Although the word "sanctuary" often refers to the temple in Jerusalem, it also refers to any place in God's creation where He dwells.

With that in mind, there is no place where we are not to praise Him. You can even praise God in a sports setting. There is no locker room too smelly nor a stadium too large in which we cannot praise God.

We can praise Him on the baseball and softball diamond, on the basketball court, and on the football field. We can praise God on a wrestling mat, on a golf course, and on the tennis court.

As an athlete, you are in His sanctuary, no matter where or what you do. There is no place on this earth where you cannot praise the Lord!

So, why praise God? Because of whom He is and the mighty things He has done.

Don't we admire and applaud the person who designs and builds great skyscrapers? Well, that person deserves our admiration and applause.

GREATER APPLAUSE

However, greater admiration and enthusiastic applause should go to our God, who has always existed and never had a beginning. Now, try to wrap your mind around that reality. You can't do it. No one can. We can grasp how life can go on for eternity, but not how something existing never had a beginning.

Greater applause should go to our God, who, by His words, created all material out of nothing.

Can you begin to count the stars above or give them names? God knows exactly how many stars there are, for He created and named them all (Psalm 147:4).

Do you know how many grains of sand are on a seashore or how many hairs are on your head? God does (Isaiah 40:12 and Matthew 10:30).

Can you simultaneously be in the United States, England, and on our moon? God is (Psalm 139:4-8). He deserves to be praised for who He is and what He has done.

So, as an athlete, how do you praise God? Our next section answers that question. As a brief introduction, Psalm 150:3-5 describes three musical instruments used in praising God. They represent the three basic classes of instruments in an orchestra: wind, stringed, and percussion.

Each musical instrument has a distinct sound and use. Each can also sound good by itself. However, all three blended together in a series of lows and highs of melodic and rhythmic sound make the most pleasant music.

1. ***When are you to praise God?***
2. ***What does it mean to praise God?***
3. ***Where are you to praise God?***
4. ***Why should you praise God?***

YOUR "ATHLETIC ORCHESTRA"

So, what does an orchestra of musical instruments have to do with you in your training sessions, practices, and competitions?

Plenty, as we will see in the rest of this chapter and the two following chapters. You can start by thinking of yourself as an orchestra for praising God through your athletic performance. Each instrument mentioned in verses 3-5 can be compared to various parts of your body.

YOUR HEART

For instance, your heart represents the trumpet in your "athletic orchestra." The trumpet is a wind instrument. It creates excitement and stirs deep emotions. The same is true of your heart. The more it is called upon to supply oxygen to your muscles, the more exciting the action of your athletic performance.

Let's say you begin an easy jog, and your heartbeat is slow and steady. There is no great excitement. Down the straightaway, you pick up the pace, and your heart responds with a faster beat. More oxygen is pumped into your muscles. Then you turn it on. You're running at top speed, and your heart pounds faster and faster. Greater is the excitement.

If your heart were an actual trumpet, the loud, clear notes would resound through the entire countryside. Every good orchestra needs the trumpet. You have one built-in to sound praises to God through your actions.

YOUR LUNGS

The harp and lyre are stringed instruments. Both require a fine touch and produce a flowing melody of notes.

The harp and lyre, or other similar stringed instruments, are necessary for an orchestra to carry the melody. They make things flow smoothly.

In your "athletic orchestra," your lungs and all that goes into your breathing can be the harp and lyre. With them, you create a flow of action that forms the smooth melody of your performance.

Like a melody is a continuous flow of notes or sounds that blend together to make a complete song, your breathing is to produce a flowing movement in your physical performance.

As she darts from sideline to sideline, the tennis player can calm herself with slower, controlled breathing. To conserve energy, she brings the melody of her performance to a slower tempo.

Every song of praise has both slow and soft music as well as a fast and harder tempo. Likewise, most athletic performances have both a slow and fast tempo.

YOUR MUSCLES

The timbrel was a percussion instrument. It added rhythm to the symphony of sounds. The timbrel, similar to the instrument we know as the tambourine, had a parchment covering either a round or square frame. Little bells or pieces of brass were fastened in the rim. It sounded like a drum with bells when hit with the hand. The timbrel accentuated feelings and emotions in the melody.

Percussion instruments, such as the timbrel, can be compared to your legs, arms, and back. They add rhythm and punctuation that flow through the melody.

Percussion instruments sound with a suddenness. They emphasize a beat. To some extent, they seem to explode. Wind instruments, like the trumpet, can create excitement. But the percussion instruments are excitement.

Your legs, arms, and back are the percussion instruments in your "athletic orchestra." A linebacker moves quickly to his left. He plants his left foot and darts powerfully to meet the on-charging running back.

Picture in slow motion the linebacker's powerful legs and lower back driving into the ball carrier while his arms wrap around him with great sounds of percussion. Contact and the loud "clanging of cymbals" are heard throughout the stadium.

YOUR BRAIN

Of course, an orchestra must have a director to oversee the perfect blending of music. And without allegiance to that director, each instrument in an orchestra would play its own music. The results would be harsh and not pleasing to the ear. A good director causes a perfect blending of rhythm and percussion throughout the music to accentuate the melody.

The director in your "athletic orchestra" is your brain. Impulses are sent from it to each instrument of your body, calling for a perfect blend of melody, rhythm, and percussion in praise of God. So, as we will see in the following two chapters, what you have stored in the library of your brain is crucial.

1. *In your "athletic orchestra," how do your heart, lungs, muscles, and brain relate to the different parts of a musical orchestra?*
2. *How can you praise God in your athletic performance?*

AN ATHLETIC PARAPHRASE

Now that we have considered how your body can be an "athletic orchestra," let's think through some ideas on praising God in this athletic paraphrase of several Bible passages.

Praise the Lord...Let your thoughts and actions shine forth to reflect the grandeur of God. Be aware of who God is. Shout the greatness of God in your every move.

Praise God in the locker room and in getting ready. Praise Him throughout each practice session and each competition. Praise Him at the training table and in the classroom. Wherever you are, praise the Lord. **Psalm 150:1**

Praise God for what He has done. Celebrate the victory you have through Jesus on the cross. God has selected you for His family. **Psalm 150:2**

Let your mind and body *sing a new song* about His greatness. **Psalm 149:1**

He knows when you go to sleep and when you awake. He understands every *thought* you have. **Psalm 139:2**

Before you speak a word, *He knows* what it will be. **Psalm 139:4**

God is everywhere at the same time. In a flash, you can go to the *depths of the sea*, and He will greet you. You can *soar to the highest of heavens,* and He is already there. *In darkness,* He sees as though it were the brightest day. **Psalm 139:7-12**

He has formed you with a perfect design to accomplish His purpose. Before you were *even in your mother's womb,* He designed your life. ***Jeremiah 1:5***

God knows the events of your life before they even happen. He designed them. His thoughts of you are *more plentiful than sand on all the seashores.* **Psalm 139:13-18**

He owns the cattle on a thousand hills. Everything that moves in the fields are His. *Psalm 50:10-11*

Look at the *stars above. God knows* their exact number *and calls each by name.* Because of His greatness, not one of them is missing. **Isaiah 40:26**

Let your mind be absorbed with His greatness. Let your body resound to His majesty. *For the Everlasting God, the Creator of all this earth,* does not tire or grow weary. He pours His strength into you. *To those who lack, He increases their power.* **Isaiah 40:28-29**

PRAISING GOD THROUGH YOUR PERFORMANCE

Let the energy flow from within, reflecting His greatness. Praise Him through your stamina. Let the melody of your song before Him be seen in the quickness of your reflexes and dexterity of your fingers.

Praise God through the rhythm of your strides. Shout His praise with perfect timing. Shout praises to the Lord with every fiber in your body.

Let His presence shine forth through you. Reflect His pureness through your athletic performance. With a performance constantly in flow with the presence of God, let it build for a great "Praise the Lord."

Sing forth your praise through your speed, quickness, dexterity, strength, stamina, and explosiveness. Let your performance sing praises to God. Shout it out with all the energy within you!

The Lord desires your praise of Him in whatever you do. It is not limited to the choir loft in a church service, nor is it limited to an expression through your athletic performance. Your praise of God is to flow through you in whatever you are doing.

As you walk and talk, praise Him through your thoughts, attitudes, and actions. Praise the Lord as you select food to eat. Praise Him as you face interruptions to a well-planned schedule.

Praise the Lord in your selection of social media, magazines, and books to read. Praise the Lord as you select which television program to watch. When relating to others, let's honor God as you are aware of His presence. You are His servant. Praise Him with all that you are and in whatever you are doing.

SCAN FOR
KINGDOM SPORTS MINUTE

SCAN FOR
CHAPTER LECTURES

CHAPTER THIRTEEN

INSIDE-OUT PRAISING GOD

In the last chapter we caught a glimpse of how you can praise God through your athletic performance. The Praise Performance is probably an entirely new athletic concept for you. In the Praise Performance you have a different goal and motivation than you normally would in your athletic performances. Your only goal is to have the attitudes, thoughts and actions of Jesus Christ. Your mind is completely controlled by the Holy Spirit, who is conforming you to the image of Christ. You have God's perspective on winning. You are more concerned about totally releasing yourself toward presenting Jesus Christ than you are with the final score. Your only motivation is to express your love for God. The Praise Performance perfectly blends all the biblical principles explained in this handbook.

One of the interesting athletic side benefits, resulting from practicing the Inside-Out Praising, is a rhythm that flows through your mind, keeping you consistently primed for a maximum performance. Staleness in any athletic performance begins with the mind. There is no room for staleness in a mind praising God for who He is and what He has done. Because this is a new way of competing, we're going to take a look at some characteristics and results of such a performance in this chapter before actually studying how to develop it in the following chapter.

PRAISE GOD WITH YOUR ATHLETIC ABILITIES

QUALITY #1 - GOD-CENTERED

You are not bothered by varying circumstances such as temperature, score, aches, the opposing team, etc. These circumstances are simply new opportunities for you to praise God through your athletic performance. You are no longer comparing yourself with performances of the past or dreams of the future. You are not overly concerned about the outcome of the contest. Your only focus throughout the performance is on God. Your only desire throughout your performance is to praise Him for who He is and what He has done.

QUALITY #2 - PURPOSEFUL PREPARATION

Although we will examine purposeful preparation more closely in the next chapter, it is one of the five qualities of each Inside-Out Praise Performance. Such preparation takes place in your mind. This characteristic is like the first one in that your attention is focused on God. It is different only in that it takes place before the actual competition begins. Before your athletic event, teammates in the locker room might be noisily stirring around you. However, your thoughts are focused on who God is and the great things He has done. By using the steps in the next chapter to develop a Praise Performance, you will see how your mind blends God's Word with Christian music.

QUALITY #3 - MAXIMIZED ABILITIES

The melody and rhythm that began in your mind accentuate your athletic skills in practice and competition. Your mind and body blend together with a fresh excitement as you run, jump, tackle, throw or whatever it is you do in your athletic performance. The height of your jump can be likened to a clashing of cymbals. The crispness of your throws emphasizes your praise of God.

QUALITY #4 - CONCERN FOR TEAMMATES

In Inside-Out Praising God, your thoughts, attitudes, and actions will lift the spirit of your entire team as you say and do things for the well-being or good of your teammates. You have a great desire to cooperate with your teammates. In your praise of God, you say and do things for the good of your teammates. Your attitudes, words and actions can lift the spirit of your entire team. We'll see how important this is in the chapter on The Perfect Team Spirit. The time might come when you will have an entire team participating in a Praise Performance of God.

QUALITY #5 - MAXIMUM ADJUSTABLE STRATEGY

You see each competition as a new opportunity to praise God with your attitudes and actions. Your opponent is not a personal enemy. He might even be a fellow Christian. Your athletic strategy, however, is geared to defeat him in the score. But your primary purpose, as you strategically attempt to defeat him, is to praise God with your attitudes and actions. Strategy is an important part of preparing for competition. If a baseball hitter's strength is a high fastball, you will want to throw him breaking pitches or keep the ball low and away. If the football running back has blazing speed to the outside, you will want to turn him in whenever he carries the football. If the one you are guarding in basketball is a deadly shot at the range of ten feet, you will want to keep him moving away from his favorite position on the court. Once your strategy has been determined, you can generate your attention to praising God with attitudes and actions that represent Jesus Christ.

Of course, you will make strategy changes during the competition. But once these are made, your attention is again focused on praising God through your attitudes and actions. Your opponent simply provides you with different types of opportunities to reflect your praise of God through your athletic performance. For instance, he might be working a strategy against you that prompts you to alter yours. He might be overly aggressive in his actions against you. You have an opportunity to endure his tactics with the attitude of Jesus as you're empowered by the Holy Spirit. But your attitude and actions are more than simply putting up with his tactics. Your attitudes and actions are a positive expression of your praise of God.

Inside-Out Praising God contains all five characteristics. You don't need to keep checking to see if they're all present. They will be if you prepare and carry out the how-tos of the next chapter.

The first part of this chapter has given you an idea of what will happen during a Praise Performance. Now let's take a look at four results of such an experience.

HUDDLE UP!

1. *Why do we call it an Inside-Out Praise Performance?*
2. *When has comparing your performance to past performances caused you problems?*
3. *Which of the five qualities of the Inside-Out Praise Performance are you the most enthused about, and why?*

THREE RESULTS OF INSIDE-OUT PRAISING

RESULT #1 - PRAISING GOD IN EVERYTHING

Inside-out praising God leads to Praising God in everything you do, including your athletic performance, prepares you for an eternity of praising God! Revelation 4:9-11 describes what our role with God in eternity will be like:

"And when the living creatures [all of nature] give glory and honor and thanks to Him [God] who sits on the throne, to Him who lives forever and ever, the twenty-four elders [all Christians including you] will fall down before the throne saying, 'Worthy art Thou, our Lord and our God, to receive glory and honor and power; for Thou didst create all things, and because of Thy will they existed, and were created.' "

Your role throughout all eternity is to praise God and do what pleases Him. Just think, your athletics can be used to help prepare you for that role.

RESULT #2 - PERSONAL RELATIONSHIP WITH GOD

Praising God in your athletic performance results in a more personal relationship with Him throughout every area of your life. Your athletic performance will no longer be isolated from the rest of your Christian life. Your praise of God will be consistent throughout all areas of your life, including your athletic performance. For instance, in athletic competition you praise God through your attitudes and actions just as you do in the classroom or in your home.

RESULT #3 - HOLY SPIRIT CONFORMS YOU

Praising God in everything you do enables you to enjoy victory and go through defeat with equal stability. You praise God in all situations, knowing that His purpose is always brought about for those who love Him and are called according to His purpose (Romans 8:28).

His purpose is for you to think and perform in the same manner as Jesus Christ as the Holy Spirit conforms you to Christ's likeness. God works all things in your life, including defeats and victories, into a perfect plan to draw recognition to Himself. Since your attention is on God and your purpose is to praise Him, you won't be shaken by a defeat or over-elated by a victory. Disappointment is the result of failing to achieve your goal. If your goal is to defeat your opponent, you will be greatly disappointed if you fail. However, if your goal is to think and act like Jesus, empowered by the Holy Spirit, you will not have such a wide range of emotions from victory to defeat. You can fully praise God on the short end of a 90-60 score in basketball just as you can in receiving a gold medal at the Olympic Games.

1. *How does giving an Inside-Out Praise Performance develop closeness with God in you?*
2. *How does giving an Inside-Out Praise Performance give you season-long stability?*
3. *How does giving an Inside-Out Praise Performance maximize your abilities?*
4. *How do the three results of an Inside-Out Praise Performance tie together?*

In your performance, as you praise God both mentally and physically, you will be doing the very thing for which you were designed. By performing the way you were designed, your athletic ability is developed to the maximum potential.

SCAN FOR
KINGDOM SPORTS MINUTE

SCAN FOR
CHAPTER LECTURES

CHAPTER FOURTEEN

YOUR INSIDE-OUT PRAISE

The this chapter, you'll learn how to develop your own Inside-Out Praise Performance. However, before you do that, consider how important your mind is to inside-out praising God.

THE 15-PENNY EXPERIENCE

This experiment will demonstrate how greatly your mind influences the actions of your body.

1. On a piece of paper, draw 15 circles, each the size of a penny. Place them as a pyramid, starting with one circle at the top and then four rows, each with one more circle than the preceding one.

2. Number each circle in the following sequence:

9

2, 15

11, 1, 8

10, 4, 14, 6

12, 3, 5, 13, 7

3. With 15 pennies in your hand, place a penny on circle #1. Continue with the second penny on circle #2. Finish placing all the pennies on the circles in numerical order up to #15, one at a time.

4. After several practice runs, time yourself.

5. Add this one variation for your second timing. As you place the pennies on the proper circles, count backward aloud and as fast as you can, from 30 to 1. Your counting backward must be fast, accurate, and without hesitation, requiring total concentration.

Most likely, even with practice, your time with the variation was slower than without it, demonstrating how your mind influences the actions of your body.

HERE'S THE POINT

Your mind can focus at 100% capacity on only one thing at a time. Since this is true, what occupies your mind during your athletic performance is extremely important. Don't you agree?

This brings us to a very important truth of the Inside-Out Praise Performance. What you are mentally thinking will influence what you are physically doing.

A mind filled with the Holy Spirit's thoughts—the same as Jesus' thoughts—will produce the Holy Spirit's actions—same as Jesus' actions. And that will keep you in close fellowship with God as He maximizes your performance.

HUDDLE UP!

1. *Explain how the 15-penny experiment affected you.*
2. *What was the point of the experiment?*
3. *How have you noticed what you are thinking can influence your performance?*

THREE INGREDIENCE OF INSIDE-OUT PRAISING

Your Inside-Out Praise Performance involves your brain (the director of your "athletic orchestra") that blends three separate ingredients—God's Word, Christian music, and a mental picture of your athletic performance. Let's look at each one.

#1 GOD'S WORD IN THE BIBLE

The Bible explains to us who God is and what He has done. And, as we have seen, He is the living centerpiece of your Inside-Out Praise Performance.

In Chapter Four, we saw that we experience the Holy Spirit at work in and through us most effectively when our mind is mentally chewing on a portion of God's Word—which are Jesus' thoughts that produce, in and through us, His actions.

Because God's Word is the foundation for your inside-out praising of God, here is a brief list of Bible passages that can help you develop the mind of Christ (1 Corinthians 2:16) with His thoughts. As you store God's Word in "your" mind, you are expanding Christ's mind in you.

I Chronicles 16:29-33, Nehemiah 9:6, Job 26:7-14, Job 37:1-13, Job 38:1-18, Job 38:25-41, Job 39:19-25, Job 39:26-30, Psalms 33:8-9, Psalms 40:5, Psalms 75:1, Psalms 86:8, Psalms 89:9, 11-12, Psalms 104, Isaiah 44:23, Isaiah 55:12, Jeremiah 32:17, I Corinthians 15:51-57, Colossians 1:16-17.

#2 CHRISTIAN MUSIC

Christian music can help connect God's Word in your mind with the physical actions needed for your athletic performance.

In Chapter 12, we thought of your body as an "athletic orchestra." In the Inside-Out Praise Performance, music coming from your "athletic orchestra" is Christian music that you have already stored in your mind.

Because the Christian music in your mind must be appropriate for connecting God's Word in your mind to the actions needed in your performance, these guidelines for choosing the appropriate music might be helpful:

1. Select only music that is honoring God. Some "Christian" music is nothing more than the beat of the world with "spiritual" words. The music you select must keep your attention on God.

2. Select only music that will highlight the portion of God's Word upon which your mind is focused.

For example, if you want to focus on creation, you will want music that builds to great peaks with perhaps the clashing of cymbals. Creation is awesome, so the music that represents it must also be awesome.

If you want to focus on the crucifixion, you will want music that is dramatic in nature. It might carry in it the sounds of agony and then perhaps build to a clashing of cymbals, denoting the death of Christ.

Of course, if you want Jesus' resurrection to be on your mind, the music ought to express victory. Again, the music you select must emphasize and highlight the portion of God's Word you have in your mind.

3. Select only music that is appropriate for actions in your athletic event. Here are some thoughts on choosing music for various sports. If your sport isn't listed, you can get an idea of how to select music from the following examples:

Baseball and softball are sports that are quiet for a while, then speed up quickly. The music should have an easy-flowing melody with an obvious rhythm. The rhythm keeps your body ready for those quick explosions of energy.

Basketball is a steady flow of action with frequent and sudden sprints. You might want music with many highs and lows to emphasize this action.

Football is dramatic and heavily accented in action. You might select music that has drums building to a peak since football is a contact sport. The clashing of cymbals would be ideal if they emphasize your focus on God's Word.

Golf requires an easy-flowing rhythm throughout your entire body. The music should have an easy-flowing melody with light accents. You want to time hitting the ball on one of those accents.

Tennis is constant, easy movements with light accents. The music you choose should reflect that action. It should have an easy-flowing melody with the proper rhythm to emphasize hitting the ball.

Wrestling is either constant movement or planning for movement. The music should have a melody and rhythm blending with various dramatic points.

Evaluate the type of physical movements involved in your sport. Then select music that will emphasize those physical movements as well as highlight the portion of God's Word in your mind.

#3 MENTAL PICTURING

On the morning of July 4, 1952, Florence Chadwick set out to be the first woman to swim the Pacific Ocean's Catalina Channel. Her route from Catalina Island to Palos Verdes on the California coast covered just over 21 miles.

The conditions on the day of her swim could not have been worse. They quickly turned her world upside-down. Not only was the water bone-chilling cold, but an unusually dense fog had settled over the ocean. The fog was so thick that Chadwick could barely see the support boats protecting her from sharks.

Nevertheless, despite the adverse conditions, she was determined to go ahead with the swim because of so much publicity.

Finally, after a grueling 15 hours and 55 minutes in the water, with her body wracked with pain and fatigue, Chadwick gave up. Unknowingly, she had called it quits less than a mile from her destination.

Later, in an interview, she told reporters that she might have kept going if the heavy fog had not made it impossible for her to have eye contact with the coastline.

After battling the elements for just shy of 16 hours, with no eye contact with her destination, Chadwick, as tough as she was, did not have the heart to keep going.

Two months later, Chadwick made a second attempt. And, unbelievably, the conditions were just as bad as they were on her first attempt. However, for her second attempt, she had prepared for the possibility of bad weather.

Each day after her training, Chadwick sat in a boat offshore with her eyes fixed on the Palos Verdes coastline. For several minutes, sitting in that boat, she used her imagination to mentally etch into her memory different "snapshots" of her destination, the coastline.

On her second attempt, despite a cold and dense fog, like the conditions two months earlier, Chadwick was able to keep going. How? By focusing her mental eyes on her "snapshots" of the Palos Verdes coastline.

Florence Chadwick's mental pictures helped her become the first woman to swim the Catalina Channel. And in the process, she smashed the existing men's record by over two hours.

In Chadwick's successful attempt, she demonstrated how what we have in our minds can determine how well we will deal with difficulties. However, let's be clear about Chadwick's mental pictures. They were mental pictures of reality, not fancy. And so must your mental pictures be—the maximum actions you can produce.

1. Why is God's Word in the Bible the foundation for each Inside-Out Praise Performance?

2. Why can Christian music be helpful in your Inside-Out Praise Performance?

3. How can you select the appropriate music for your sport?

4. How does what Florence Chadwick experienced tie in with Jesus' practice of telling stories to His listeners?

5. How might mental picturing of your inside-out praise performance help you experience it?

6. Explain how all three ingredients—God's Word, Christian music, and mental picturing—work together to help you experience the Spirit of Christ in you, praising His Father through your athletic performance.

JESUS THE MASTER STORY TELLER

As we know, Jesus was a master storyteller. His stories activated the imagination of His listeners to engage them in the truth He was teaching.

In fact, in the first four New Testament books of Matthew, Mark, Luke, and John, Jesus told over 50 different stories, known as parables. Each activated the mind of his listeners.

In the Inside-Out Praise Performance, as vividly as you can, you mentally picture what actions you will take during your performance—running, jumping, throwing, blocking, hitting, etc.

As we have seen from Florence Chadwick's example and Jesus' practice—along with the 15-penny experiment at the beginning of this chapter—what we have in our mind greatly influences what we do.

Now, once you have run your actions through your mind a few times, do it several more times connected with the music and God's Word. Of course, this will require lots of practice. But the experience will be worth it: Close fellowship with God Himself, stability—or consistency—and maximizing your abilities.

SCAN FOR
KINGDOM SPORTS MINUTE

SCAN FOR
CHAPTER LECTURES

CHAPTER FIFTEEN

BIBLICAL-ISOLATION

"I'm past it, but I'm not over it. I don't think I'll ever be." Those were the words of the Atlanta Falcons' head coach, Dan Quinn, a few weeks after his National Football League team lost the 2017 Super Bowl to the New England Patriots, 34-28.

That score would normally indicate a close, hard-fought game that most football coaches would eventually get over.

WASN'T CLOSE MOST OF THE GAME

However, Coach Quinn was having a more difficult time than normal in getting over the outcome because his team was leading 28-3 midway through the third quarter and even 28-12 in the fourth quarter with only 5:56 left on the clock.

The Patriots tied the score as the fourth quarter ended, and they won in overtime on their first possession, capping the greatest comeback in Super Bowl history.

So, what happened?

In most athletic contests, it is not the physical mistakes by themselves that hurt the most. It's the effect those mistakes have on an athlete's mind. And, as we saw in our last chapter, what we have in our mind influences our actions. Negative thoughts produce negative actions, and negative actions produce negative results.

So, unless an athlete or team can isolate the mistake—setting it apart from the present—that mistake can cause a downward spiral in physical actions because of the negative thoughts it produces.

On the other hand, if an athlete or team is far behind in the score—as the Patriots were—and if they isolate the past by focusing only on the present, they can come back in the score. Again, by focusing only on the present.

ONE PLAY AT A TIME

Going into the second half, Josh McDaniels, the Patriots' offensive coordinator, asked his running backs: "Do you believe we're going to win? I do, too. Let's just play our best half. I don't want you to do anything you can't do. Don't try to make it all up in one play. Just play each play by itself."

On the final drive to tie the score before regulation time ended, Patriots wide receiver Julian Edelman made perhaps the most "impossible" catch when Tom Brady's pass caromed off three Falcon players into his diving and outstretched hands.

Patriots running back LeGarrette Blount shouted to his teammates, confirming what they already believed: "We got Tom Brady. We got Tom Brady. We get into OT, and it's over."

From a 16-point deficit with less than six minutes remaining, isolating each play by focusing only on the present play, the Patriots did get into overtime. And, with their quarterback, Tom Brady, who many consider the greatest quarterback of all time, the Patriots defeated the Atlanta Falcons. A loss that the Falcons' coach, Dan Quinn, had a hard time isolating.

HUDDLE UP!

1. *Referring to both the Atlanta Falcons and New England Patriots, how does the 2017 Super Bowl illustrate the need for practicing isolation in training sessions, practices, and competitions?*
2. *Explain how Philippians 3:13-14 is the premise for biblical isolation.*
3. *How do "turning points" affect a competition?*

PREMISE FOR BIBLICAL-ISOLATION

One of the concepts God has imparted to us through the apostle Paul is the concept of isolation. In biblical-isolation, you isolate the past from your mind by totally concentrating on your goal—focus on Jesus as you yield to the Holy Spirit to live out the life of Jesus in and through your thoughts, attitudes, and actions.

The apostle Paul wrote:

> *"Brethren, I do not regard myself as having laid hold of it yet,* ***but one thing I do: forgetting what lies behind*** *and reaching forward to what lies ahead, I press toward the goal for the prize of the upward call of God in Christ Jesus."*
> **Philippians 3:13-14**

The phrase "in Christ Jesus" means to be in a mental and spiritual union, or oneness, with Jesus. Paul forgot the past by mentally focusing on oneness with Jesus.

That's biblical-isolation.

"TURNING POINTS" AFFECT MENTAL ATTITUDE

Certain happenings in an athletic contest become known as turning points because they can have such a devastating impact on your mental attitude. And your mental attitude influences your actions, which can cause a significant change in the competition.

For example, in a tennis match, the score of the first set is two games to one in favor of your opponent. In the fourth game, your opponent smashes a ball toward the center of the net. The ball hits the top of the net and barely drops on your side. It's impossible for you to reach the ball.

Your opponent wins the game. But, more importantly, instead of the set being tied two games to two, it is now three games to one. You're down two games. If you develop a defeated attitude such as, "I'll never win now," it can be said that your opponent's dribbled shot was the turning point in that set.

LEAVING THE PAST IN THE PAST

Your natural tendency might be to allow past negative experiences to influence your current actions. Yet, the apostle Paul had a different way of dealing with the past. He mentally left it completely in the past. Paul's only goal was always in the present—union, or oneness, with Jesus.

The word Paul used for *"forgetting"* in Philippians 3:13-14 means that he totally forgot. His past and the events that had just happened were no longer in his mind.

Kenneth Wuest, in his Word Studies in the Greek New Testament, says Paul used an illustration of a Greek runner. The athlete is running all out and isn't concerned with his opponents running behind him. He doesn't allow their footsteps, near or far, to detract him from what he is doing. He has completely "forgotten" them.

HOW TO BIBLICALLY ISOLATE

Remember the biblical premise for isolation in athletic perfection that we looked at earlier. In fact, in reviewing it, let's look at a few keywords:

"Brethren, I do not regard myself as having laid hold of it yet,
***but one thing I do: forgetting what lies behind** and reaching*
forward to what lies ahead, I press toward the goal for the prize
of the upward call of God in Christ Jesus."
Philippians 3:13-14

"FORGETTING"

So, how do you forget about an error or a strikeout? How do you forget about the fumble in football that gave the other team good field position? How do you forget the height and skill of players on the opposing basketball team? How do you forget about how badly you were beaten by your opponent the last time you met? How do you leave the past in the past?

"REACHING FORWARD"

You do it the same way the apostle Paul did. He reached *"forward to what lies ahead!"*

"Reaching forward" is an athletic term that describes an athlete riveting his full attention on a specific goal. As the athlete does this with all his conscious effort, his physical abilities are drawn to that goal.

For instance, as the Greek runner runs toward the finish line, his eyes are focused sharply on the cord stretched across the track. All he can think about is getting there as fast as his abilities can take him. He's not distracted. His eyes never move from the finish line. The athlete is running full speed forward, following the focus of his eyes.

Paul's riveted his mental eyes on Jesus.

"PRESS ON"

Then, in Paul's next words, he told of the concentrated effort he used to reach his goal. He wrote, *"I press on toward the goal..."* The word "press" means to pursue—to actively go after something. It reveals the intensity with which Paul reached toward his goal.

"TOWARD"

The word *"toward"* implies bearing down upon the goal. Paul pursued his goal, bearing down upon it with his total energy. His only life goal was to be in union, or oneness, with Jesus.

Each situation in your athletic performance is an opportunity for you to also be in a union, or oneness, with Jesus as you focus on Him, yielding to the Holy Spirit to produce His thoughts, attitudes, and actions in and through you.

But you will not automatically forget about a negative or positive situation—as the Falcons and Patriots had an opportunity to do—by just saying, "I won't think about it anymore."

That's a non-workable, negative approach. It's like saying you won't think about a blue elephant. Paul took the positive approach. He kept his mental eyes on Christ.

1. *What is an example from your competition of failing to "forget" an error or mistake?*
2. *Why is it difficult to put distractions behind us in sports?*
3. *Using Philippians 3:13-14, how can you biblically isolate in your training sessions, practices, and competitions?*

BIBLICAL ISOLATION ILLUSTRATED

The 15-penny experiment in our last chapter should have convinced you that your mind can focus, at 100% capacity, on only one thing at a time. The more you concentrate on allowing the Holy Spirit to express Jesus Christ in your thoughts, attitudes, and actions, the less influence a negative situation will have on your mind.

A GOLFING EXAMPLE

Let's say that, as a golfer, you drive the ball to a good position in the middle of the fairway. Walking off the tee, you feel good about your drive. Your natural attitude is great. But on your next shot, using a seven iron, you dribble the ball barely 40 yards. Now, your natural attitude isn't so good, is it?

You're disappointed with yourself. Consequently, you're a little careless on the next shot because you're still thinking about the missed shot with the seven iron. So, how would you handle this situation using the concept of isolation?

Walking off the tee, you start mentally preparing for the seven-iron shot. You are thinking that your approach and execution of the shot are opportunities for you to inside-out praise God.

Because of your focus, the Holy Spirit might bring a portion of God's Word to your mind that relates to your present situation. However, even with your focus on Jesus, along with a passage and music running through your mind, you dub the seven-iron shot.

Now, what do you do? You practice isolation following this failure, just as you practiced isolation when you hit your great tee shot.

For a moment, you learn from whatever mistake you made in hitting the fairway ball. If your inside elbow was away from your body, you'll want to keep it tighter. Or, if your back-swing was too fast, you'll want to slow it down.

Once you learn from the bad shot, you mentally prepare for your next shot. It's your next opportunity to inside-out praise God on a beautiful course, as the Holy Spirit conforms you to the likeness of Jesus Christ.

NO LONG-TERM DISAPPOINTMENT

By successfully practicing biblical isolation, you will never be disappointed for long stretches since you will always be pursuing your one perfect goal—God's goal for you.

Notice from this golfing illustration that you practice isolation following every shot, whether good or bad. The same is true in every training session, practice, and competition.

DIFFERENT RESULTS?

What do you suppose would have happened if the Atlanta Falcons had been practicing isolation? We can only surmise. But because of their huge lead with less than six minutes to play in regulation, it's safe to say that the results would probably have been different.

Of course, biblical-isolation described in this chapter can only be successfully applied by the Christian athlete. It deals with your focus on Jesus and His Spirit in you (Romans 8:29), one play at a time. One shot at a time. One situation at a time. And always in the present.

SCAN FOR
KINGDOM SPORTS MINUTE

SCAN FOR
CHAPTER LECTURES

CHAPTER SIXTEEN

OVERCOMING "SETBACKS"

The possibility of having an athletic setback strikes fear in the minds of most athletes. A setback is any situation that causes your progress to start reversing…or, at least, be halted.

You train long and hard for a particular competition only to have an injury, poor grades, illness, or some other circumstance deprive you of the opportunity to compete.

In this chapter, by looking at a situation through God's eyes, a situation we would ordinarily call a setback is not a setback at all.

GOD DOESN'T SEE "SETBACKS" AS SETBACKS

God's perspective on "setbacks" differs from how we see them. Interestingly, Jesus never promised a life free from difficult situations. However, He did promise He would see us through every difficulty.

"These things I have spoken to you, that in Me you may have peace.
In the world, you have tribulation [e.g., physical injury, breakdown of communication, defeat, etc.], *but take courage; I have overcome the world."*
John 16:33 [Brackets are added.]

In Jesus' bold statement, His word, "peace," implies rest. It refers to the absence of inner tension. Like relaxing in a hammock by a still lake on a lazy day. Notice that Jesus used the word "peace" in the same verse that He used the word "tribulation."

"Tribulation" is a happening full of pressure and distress. As you can see, "peace" and "tribulation" have opposite meanings. Jesus was speaking about a person who had no tension in a tension-packed situation. Now, whether you have peace in tribulation depends on your perspective.

SETBACK OR OPPORTUNITY

Allen Gallagher, an offensive tackle on the 1972 University of Southern California football team, had dreamed of playing in the Rose Bowl. He earned a starting spot on what was to become the Number One team in the country. It looked as though his dream would come true.

Then it happened. A knee injury in a non-conference game required surgery, and Gallagher was out for the rest of the regular season. Dream shattered.

Gallagher had two ways he could view his difficult situation. He could view it from his own natural perspective and see the injury as a major setback, a huge stumbling block to not only his Rose Bowl dream but also to a future professional career.

On the other hand, he could view his knee injury from God's perspective and see it as an opportunity to rely on God for whatever purpose He had in mind.

Gallagher told me, "As a football player, I felt the worst thing that could happen to me would be to get hurt. But this year, that's what happened. And yet, because of my relationship with Christ, I saw my injury as a steppingstone to becoming a better player and stronger person, rather than as a tragedy."

In practices, Gallagher was on the field encouraging his teammates. Throughout the season, they noticed his positive attitude, and several wanted to learn more about this Jesus that meant so much to him.

Amazingly, and in line with God's purpose, Gallagher mended and was able to play in the Rose Bowl. In the NFL draft, the New England Patriots drafted him to play professional football.

HOW TO SEE "SETBACKS" THROUGH GOD'S EYES

Here's the thing. As a Christian athlete, you are not immune from difficulties that many would call setbacks. However, as you keep your mental eyes on Jesus, even thinking of Him in your body experiencing the situation and praising His Father, God will enable you to see the situation through His eyes.

James wrote to hurting fellow believers:

"Consider it all joy, my brethren, when you encounter various trials, knowing that the testing of your faith produces endurance. And let endurance have its perfect result, that you may be perfect and complete, lacking in nothing."
James 1:2-4

CONSIDER TRIALS

The word "consider," implies viewing—or mentally picturing—something a certain way. And the word "trials" refers to anything that tests your reliance on God. It can be an emotional disturbance, a family crisis, an injury, relationship trouble, etc. Anything at all...which, of course, includes anything that could be called an athletic setback.

Now, how are we to consider a trial? God tells us through James to consider—or mentally picture—a trial as a vehicle of joy. "Consider it all joy," James wrote.

JOY IS GLADNESS

The word "joy" does not refer to happiness. God is not telling us to be happy when we have a trial. The word "joy" refers to gladness.

So, what's the difference between gladness and happiness? Happiness is an upbeat feeling that is always based on circumstances.

You are happy when you fulfill your dream of playing in the Rose Bowl. You are not happy with a knee injury that can cause you to miss out on the Rose Bowl and, possibly, a pro football career.

If circumstances like an undefeated season, no injuries, good statistics, etc., are favorable, you're happy. If they're not, you're unhappy. Happiness is an emotion stirred in us when the right circumstances happen.

However, gladness is an attitude. It has nothing to do with our circumstances.

Okay, you might be thinking, *Wait a minute. I can't be glad when our baseball team just lost a playoff game we needed for the championship.*

You're right. It isn't natural to be glad in such a situation. It's supernatural…Christlike.

REASON FOR JOY

In James 1:2-4, God tells us the reason for Jesus' joy, or attitude of gladness. He says that the testing of faith, or our reliance on God, produces endurance—a toughness of spiritual resolve to rely on God for whatever He chooses to do.

And here's the thing. The testing of our faith produces more faith. Like testing or exercising, our muscles produce more strength and endurance in our muscles.

Testing leads to completeness, a greater union with Jesus. That's why you can have joy or be glad after losing a playoff game. Your goal is being accomplished. Jesus is living through you, and you are becoming more like Him.

1. ***In this chapter, why does the word "setback" often have quotation marks?***
2. ***Describe some of your athletic "setbacks" and their effect on you.***
3. ***Discuss the meaning and implications of the following verses and how they apply to your athletic performance.***

   John 16:23
   James 1:2-4
   Romans 5:3-5
   Romans 8:28-29
   2 Corinthians 12:9-10
   1 Thessalonians 5:1

NO SUCH THING AS AN ATHLETIC SETBACK

From God's perspective, there is no such thing as an athletic setback. Situations that we often call setbacks are really opportunities to rely on God to develop into mature Christlikeness, a person who totally relies on his eternal Father.

THE PROGRESS IN PAUL

God allowed the apostle Paul to encounter several situations through which Paul developed a deeper trust in Him. Paul was shipwrecked, imprisoned, stoned, beaten, etc. What was Paul's attitude in each of *these difficult circumstances?*

"We also exult in our tribulations; ***knowing that tribulation brings about perseverance; and perseverance, proven character, and proven character, hope; and hope*** *does not disappoint, because the love of God has been poured out within our hearts through the Holy Spirit who was given to us."*
Romans 5:3-5

Again, what did Paul do about situations that many would call setbacks? He exulted in them. What…he didn't complain?

No complaining. In fact, just the opposite. The word "exult" means that Paul boasted about his circumstances. He didn't gripe. He wasn't depressed by them. He didn't feel bad about them.

That's strange, isn't it? It's natural to be mentally and emotionally down when you're in the jaws of a miserable situation. But remember, as a Christian, you aren't to live a natural life. You are to live a supernatural life in union with Jesus. His supernatural life is in you and flows through you (Galatians 2:20).

Paul knew that each tribulation—difficult situation—would help develop him into the complete Christlike man that God desired him to be for assignments that God had for him (Ephesians 2:10).

PERSEVERANCE

Paul wrote that tribulations—or so-called setbacks—produce perseverance. That's a bearing up under a burden. "Perseverance" is the same Greek word James used in James 1:3 for "endurance."

PROVEN CHARACTER

But it didn't stop there. Paul wrote that perseverance—endurance—brings about proven character. Proven character describes someone who has gone through a testing and who has been approved.

In other words, Paul stood the test; God approved Paul in how he handled his "setbacks."

God will also approve of how you keep your mental eyes on Jesus in dealing with a "setback," yielding to the Holy Spirit to express Jesus' reliance on His Father, trusting Him to carry out His purpose for it.

HOPE

Proven character leads to the next stage of development in a Christian. It produces hope. And hope is the expectation of something good in the future. What is the hope? Here's how Paul explained it:

"And we know that God causes all things to work together for good to those who love God, to those who are called according to His purpose" (Romans 8:28).

From this passage, we understand that God causes or allows something to happen for His purpose! He is in total control.

"SETBACKS" ARE OPPORTUNITIES

A situation other people might describe as a setback is an opportunity to see God work according to His plan for your life. Like He did in Allen Gallegher's football days at USC. Because athletics are a vital part of your life, you can be sure that God will work through your training sessions, practices, and competitions to conform you to the image of His Son.

Paul continued by saying that hope does not disappoint. That's important to remember. Hope does not disappoint because God has a purpose for every difficult situation.

Here's how The Living Bible paraphrases Paul's words in **Romans 3:3-5**.

"We can rejoice, too, when we run into problems and trials, for we know that they are good for us—they help us learn to be patient.

"And patience develops strength of character in us and helps us trust God more each time until finally our hope and faith are strong and steady.

"Then, when that happens, we will be able to hold our heads high no matter what happens and know that all is well, for we will know how dearly God loves us, and we will feel this warm love everywhere within us because God has given us the Holy Spirit to fill our hearts with His love."

CRUCIFIXION: DEFEAT OR STEPPINGSTONE

God is telling us that what we often see as a defeat, He sees as a steppingstone to His victory. For instance, it was natural for onlookers to see the crucifixion of Jesus Christ as a defeat. His shoulders were dislocated. His back was torn open from the scourging. His face was badly beaten.

Most of His friends had deserted Him. No one spoke up in His defense. Curious bystanders mocked Him as He hung in agony. Even His disciples thought the end had come.

But from God's viewpoint, the beginning had just begun. The natural viewpoint saw weakness. God saw power. The natural viewpoint saw defeat. God saw victory.

LOOK FOR GOD'S PURPOSE

Your natural reaction to a situation is looking on the surface…at the circumstances and reacting to them. But Jesus looks through the circumstances and sees His Father's purpose.

Can you imagine our predicament concerning eternity if the crucifixion had not taken place? Paying the penalty for our sins would still be up to us. We would have to pay own penalty by dying an eternal death—***"The wages of sin is death…"*** **Romans 6:23**. And we couldn't do it.

The crucifixion—or "setback"—also had to happen before the victorious resurrection could happen. Without the crucifixion, there would be no resurrection.

From our natural viewpoint, what we often see as a defeat is the preparatory stages through which God will demonstrate His power.

GIDEON'S CHALLENGE

These three facts of Judges 7 give us a graphic illustration:

1. God called Gideon to lead Israel into battle against the Midianites.

2. Gideon rounded up an army of 33,000 men to battle against an army of 135,000.

3. God told Gideon that he had too many men.

"And the Lord said to Gideon, '***The people who are with you are too many for me to give Midian into their hands, lest Israel become boastful saying, 'My own power has delivered me'.***"
Judges 7:2

4. Gideon's army was finally cut back to only 300 men.

5. The result? God, through 300 men, defeated an army of 135,000 trained soldiers.

6. Why only 300 men? God received all the glory. He turned certain defeat into victory.

PAUL'S CHALLENGE

God demonstrates His power through human weakness.

The apostle Paul was bothered by a physical ailment. Although he asked God three times to remove it, God did not remove Paul's ailment. Through this experience, Paul wrote about God's perspective.

*"And He has said to me, '****My grace is sufficient for you, for power is perfected in weakness.****' Most gladly, therefore, will I rather boast about my weaknesses, that the power of Christ may dwell in me.* ***Therefore, I am well content with weaknesses, with insults, with distresses, with persecutions, with difficulties, for Christ's sake; for when I am weak, then I am strong.***"
2 Corinthians 12:9-10

1. *Explain how "setbacks" are both opportunities and steppingstones for the Christian athlete.*
2. *What three facts tell us God looks beyond our athletics?*
3. *For a Christian athlete, why is there no such thing as an athletic setback?*

GOD LOOKS BEYOND ATHLETICS

The following biblical facts will give you God's perspective on every difficult situation that, from a natural perspective, people would consider to be an athletic setback.

Fact #1 - God's goal for you is that you take on the likeness of Jesus Christ.

"For whom He foreknew, He also predestined to become conformed to the image of His Son, that He might be the first-born among many brethren."
Romans 8:29

Fact #2 - God will cause everything, including situations that could be termed athletic setbacks, to work together in building Christlikeness in you.

***"And we know that God causes all things to work together for good to those who love God,** to those who are called according to His purpose."*
Romans 8:28

Fact #3 - God desires you to thank Him for every situation. You can sincerely do this, knowing that God will use every trial to form the likeness of Christ in you for different assignments He has for you.

"... ***In everything, give thanks;*** for this is God's will for you in Christ Jesus."
1 Thessalonians 5:18

***"For we are his workmanship, created in Christ Jesus for good works,** which God prepared beforehand, that we should walk in them."*
Ephesians 2:10

GOD CARRIES OUT HIS PURPOSE

At the National Collegiate Weightlifting Championships, my friend had a good chance to set a record in one of the lifts. However, he was unable to succeed with even his starting poundage. Consequently, he failed to place in the contest.

However, my friend looked at his failure from God's perspective. He didn't understand why he was unable to succeed with a poundage he had previously lifted with ease. Yet, he felt confident that God caused or allowed his failure for a purpose.

That night, when he phoned his parents, at first, they thought he had won because of the enthusiasm still in his voice. Sometime later, his father asked how he could be so content after failing to place in the most important contest of his life.

My friend then shared with his father how Jesus had given him a perspective of trusting God for the results. God used this athlete's attitude toward failure to help his father see the reality of Jesus Christ in his life. Not long after that conversation, his father turned his life over to Jesus and became one of His followers.

God accomplished one of His purposes—bringing my friend's father to Himself—through a "failure" in a weightlifting contest.

God allows every trial that comes your way for a reason. He is concerned about you reaching your true goal for living—to focus on Jesus, yielding to the Holy Spirit to live Jesus in and through your thoughts, attitudes, and actions, even in dealing with what others would call an athletic setback.

SCAN FOR
KINGDOM SPORTS MINUTE

SCAN FOR
CHAPTER LECTURES

CHAPTER SEVENTEEN

THE ATHLETE-COACH RELATIONSHIP

When I was in competitive weightlifting, a renowned coach agreed to train me for the upcoming state championships. Although I had trained myself for many years, I knew this man would be able to help improve my technique. He had creative ideas on how an athlete should train to get top results.

The evening came for my first workout with him. After warming up, I asked my coach what he wanted me to do. He told me to begin power snatching. That's pulling the weight from my waist all the way overhead in one movement.

After doing several repetitions, my shoulders began to hurt due to the wide hand spacing used in this lift. I told my coach about the pain and thought I should practice a different lift that would put less stress on my shoulders.

I'll never forget the surprised and unsympathetic look he gave me. He knew there was no injury to my shoulders. It was just the pain of lifting weights to an overhead position with tired arms and shoulders.

His reply to my request was straight to the point. "I told you to do the power snatch," he said, "and that's what I want you to do. Now get with it."

My natural reaction was to tell him a few things I thought he should learn about coaching and stomp off to the locker room. Instead, the Holy Spirit immediately brought two very important biblical concepts to my mind.

First, I remembered my responsibility in the chain of command. Second, I remembered the attitude God wanted me to have as I carried out my responsibility.

THE ATHLETE'S CHAIN OF COMMAND

God has placed the athlete in a chain of command—a line of authority—that always has at least one leader and one follower.

For example, the head coach of a team is the leader, and each player is a follower. A chain of command can also have more than one leader. A football team has a head coach and several assistant coaches. Each assistant coach is a leader of players and a follower in relation to the head coach.

The line of authority, then, of a football team would be the head coach, assistant coaches, team captains, and the rest of the players.

BASED ON THE BIBLE

The chain of command is a biblical concept designed by God to help us function at our maximum effectiveness. In such a line of authority, there is a minimum of confusion.

God's chain-of-command is based on: Genesis 3:16; I Corinthians 11:3; Romans 13:1-2; Ephesians 5:23; 6:1; 6:5-9; Colossians 3:18-20; 3:22; Titus 3:1 and I Peter 2:13-15.

CHAIN OF COMMAND IN ACTION

When my coach told me to continue practicing the lift that caused my shoulders to ache, I realized that my role in the chain of command was to obey his instructions. It didn't matter if I agreed with his approach or not. As long as he was my coach, his responsibility was to give me instructions, and my responsibility was to follow them.

The same is true in your responsibility to your coach. You might not agree on every point, but your role is to focus on Jesus and yield to the Holy Spirit to live out through you Jesus' submissiveness. We'll look at His submissiveness later in this chapter.

THE DOULOS ROLE

When I returned to the lifting platform to practice the same lift, I could have simply gone through the motions, silently grumbling. Of course, if I had done that, the purpose of the practice session would have been wasted for the most part…to prepare for the upcoming state championships.

However, I returned to practice the lift with a new enthusiasm; I was determined to do it my coach's way. An athlete who has a determination to do it their coach's way could be described as a "doulos" athlete.

My weightlifting workout was excellent because I understood my role in the athletic chain of command and viewed myself as a doulos athlete. I didn't even notice the discomfort to my shoulders when I had the doulos attitude.

PAUL'S RELATIONSHIP WITH JESUS

So, what is a doulos athlete?

Paul used the word "doulos" (due loss) frequently to describe his relationship with Jesus. "Doulos" is the Greek word for bondservant. Paul wrote in **Romans 1:1**, ***"Paul, a bondservant of Christ Jesus, called as an apostle, set apart for the gospel of God…"***

The word "doulos" is taken from another Greek word, "deo," which means "to bind." The doulos is bound to another person. Their will is completely swallowed up in the will of the other person.

YOUR COACH'S INSTRUCTIONS

Often, an athlete's natural response to a command he disagrees with is stubbornness. He might go through the motions of carrying out the command from his coach, but his heart isn't in it.

However, a doulos athlete's will is bound to his coach's command. If his coach yells, "Jump!" the doulos athlete doesn't waste time asking, "Why?" He immediately puts everything into the jump.

Now, we can contrast the word "doulos" with "therapon," another Greek word for servant. The therapon has a choice in whether he wants to carry out the command. If he doesn't like it, he can always quit.

The doulos has no choice. He is completely at the disposal of the person for whom he is a doulos. Any desire on his leader's part results in instant action by the doulos. "Doulos" is the word Paul used to describe his responsiveness to God. Any desire on God's part became instant action on Paul's part.

My weightlifting workout went so well when I returned to the platform to lift because I looked upon myself as a doulos to my coach. I wanted my actions to be the instant and complete response to my coach's desire for me. I knew that by being obedient to my coach, I was also being obedient to God.

"Servants, be submissive to your masters with all respect... for this finds favor with God."
1 Peter 2:18-20

YOUR FOLLOWERSHIP ROLE

A chain-of-command operates at 100% efficiency only when each person in a "followership" role looks upon themself as a doulos, or bondservant, to their leader.

As a doulos athlete, you are in a "followership" role to your coach, the leader. Your will is completely swallowed up in the will of your coach.

THE DOULOS ROLE OF JESUS

Jesus demonstrated total submissiveness to His Father throughout His entire life. It was most notable for us in the Garden of Gethsemane shortly before Roman soldiers took Him captive. Jesus had left three of His disciples at the garden entrance. He took three of His men a little further into the garden, where He slumped to the ground in agony.

"Abba, Father," He prayed, "all things are possible for you. Remove this cup from me. ***Yet not what I will, but what you will."***
Mark 14:36

NOT WHAT I WILL

Initially, although Jesus had a desire to go through with His Father's plan, He didn't want to experience the torturous crucifixion or the painful separation from His Father.

But Jesus had the attitude of a doulos when He told His Father, "Yet not what I will, but what you will." A short time later, Jesus subjected Himself to the crucifixion.

EXPRESSING YOUR CONCERNS

In the same way, Jesus expressed His desire to His Father, as a doulos athlete, you have the right to go to your coach and express your concerns. And, like Jesus, your doulos attitude is to do what your coach tells you to do wholeheartedly.

Jesus was the perfect doulos. He was in instant and complete obedience to His Father. His greatest desire was to accomplish His Father's purpose, to take our place on the cross in paying for our sins.

His Father's desire was Jesus' action. He released His entire self toward carrying out His Father's plan, even when it meant a torturous death.

1. *What is the chain of command, and why has God given it to us?*
2. *Describe the different chains of command within which you function.*
3. *What is a doulos athlete, and how does that role apply to your athletic performance?*
4. *Contrast the "therapon" and "doulos" athlete and discuss the effect each would have on a team.*
5. *In what way do you, as a doulos athlete, have a right to go to your coach to question an assignment (Mark 14:36)?*

YOUR RESPONSIBILITY AMPLIFIED

Hopefully, the following six questions and answers concerning your relationship with your coach will help you understand the implications of being a doulos athlete.

QUESTION #1

Is your coach responsible for letting you know the details of their motives, strategy, or any other area that affects you as an athlete?

No, your coach is responsible to their leader for your care in practices and competitions. However, your coach is not responsible for relating everything to you. Coaches can choose to communicate with their team that way, but they do not have the responsibility to do so. They would have that responsibility only if their leader instructed them to do so.

You might have some consolation in that even Jesus did not know every detail of His Father's plan. When His disciples questioned Him concerning the exact time of His return, He replied:

"But concerning that day or that hour, no one knows, not even the angels in heaven, nor the Son, but only the Father" (Mark 13:32).

QUESTION #2

What if your coach is not a good doulos to the authorities in their chain of command? Does that release you from your doulos responsibility?

No, it doesn't.

Peter wrote in **I Peter 2:18-20,**

> *"Servants, be submissive to your masters with all respect,* ***not only to those who are good and gentle but also to those who are unreasonable.*** *For this finds favor if, for the sake of conscience toward God, a man bears up under sorrows when suffering unjustly. For what credit is there if you endure it with patience when you sin and are harshly treated? But if, when you do what is right and suffer for it, you patiently endure it, this finds favor with God."*

QUESTION #3

If you think you know more than your coach in a particular area, is it right to do what you think is best rather than what your coach says?

No, it isn't. One thing to keep in mind is that any time God chooses to do so, He could change the thinking of your coach. God did so with Pharaoh when it served His best interest (Exodus 8-12).

If God does not choose to change your coach's thinking, He will use it for a reason He has in mind. Your responsibility is to carry out your coach's commands and desires no matter how knowledgeable you are.

QUESTION #4

Does God want you to be a doulos athlete even when your coach makes mistakes in judgment and relating to the team?

Yes, He does. Keep in mind that coaches are responsible to the authority above them. If their authority decides they make too many mistakes, they can be replaced. You are still responsible for being a doulos athlete even when your coach makes bad judgments or relates to the team poorly.

QUESTION #5

What should you do if you think your coach is doing a poor job, but the authority above won't replace them?

That's a concern for the authority above your coach. It should not weigh on your mind. When we take on responsibilities and concerns that God has not given us in the chain of command, our mind becomes encumbered with unnecessary weight. Your effectiveness as an athlete will increase as you learn to mentally let go of concerns that do not fall within your realm of responsibility.

QUESTION #6

As a doulos athlete, what should your response be if your coach gives you instructions that violate God's Word in the Bible?

Unfortunately, each chain of command potentially has leaders who do not listen to God for their instructions. Occasionally, they will give a command without really being aware that it violates God's Word.

If this happens, go to your coach and share your concern about how their instructions affect you as a Christian. Be sure to do this in an understanding manner so as not to accuse your coach of being against God.

For example, you might say, "Coach, because of my faith, I've got a problem with.... Can we talk about it?"

Remember, most likely, your coach didn't give you the instructions to oppose God. However, because your coach does have a reason, try to discern what that reason is.

GO DEEP

1. ***Discuss each of the six questions and answers concerning obedience to your coach and the implications they have for you as a doulos athlete.***
2. ***How can you, as a doulos athlete, contribute to your coach's leadership?***

THE DANIEL APPROACH

You might even offer your coach another course of action that would fulfill the instructions. In the Old Testament, Daniel is a model for us in this approach. According to Daniel 1:8-16, here's what happened.

THE KING'S ORDERS

Daniel was in captivity. The king ordered him and other young men to eat certain rich foods. Daniel knew the food was not God's choice for him, so he offered another course of action. He discerned that the king's command was given for all the young men to eat the rich food to make them strong and healthy.

DANIEL'S REQUEST

Daniel presented another approach that would accomplish what the king wanted and keep within God's guidelines. He requested permission for him and his friends to eat their chosen food for ten days.

If, after ten days, they were not stronger and healthier than the other young men, then they would eat whatever they were ordered to eat.

THE KING'S DECISION

The king granted Daniel's request. He allowed Daniel and his friends to eat their food for ten days. After ten days, Daniel and his friends were found to be stronger and healthier than the other men. From that time onward, they were exempt from eating the king's food and were allowed to eat according to their convictions.

AN EXTREME SITUATION FOR YOU

Let's say your coach gives you an order to deliberately rough up a player on the other team. After you let your coach know that, as a Christian, you have a problem carrying out those instructions, you suggest a possible alternate course of action to accomplish the purpose.

For the sake of illustration, let's assume that your coach's reason for such instructions was to quickly remove from the game an opposing athlete who was very effective against your team.

You offer your coach a possible strategy of nullifying this athlete's effectiveness while keeping within the rules. If your coach accepts or decides against the original instructions, your proposal was well worth it.

On the other hand, let's say your coach still insists on you carrying out the original instructions. Because that violates God's way of doing it, you're in a difficult situation. If you tell your coach you can't follow those orders, you could be benched and even dropped from the team.

In Acts 4:18, Peter and John were ordered not to talk to anybody about Jesus. That order clearly violated Jesus' command in Matthew 28:18-20 for His followers to teach about Him everywhere.

So, Peter and John responded, "Whether it is right in the sight of God to give heed to you rather than to God, you be the judge: for we cannot stop speaking what we have seen and heard" (Acts 4:19-20).

YOUR TOP RESPONSIBILITY

If you do as your coach orders, you will not be focusing on Jesus and yielding to the Holy Spirit to express Jesus in and through you. So, what do you do?

Your top responsibility is to obey God's Word. You can say something like, "I'm sorry, coach. I want to give you everything I have, but I can't carry out those instructions."

God is in complete charge of the situation. If He has a future for you in athletics, nothing can stop it…even if you are cut from the team.

KEEP IN MIND

Three Facts

1. God is intensely interested in you.

"But the very hairs of your head are all numbered." **Matthew 10:30**

2. God has given you abilities for a purpose.

"The Lord has made everything for its (His) own purpose…" **Proverbs 16:4**

3. God works every circumstance toward His purpose as you yield to Him.

In the following verse purpose is to conform us to the likeness of Jesus. Sometimes, He even uses the "sandpaper" of a coach's ungodly instructions.

"And we know that for those who love God, all things work together for good, for those who are called according to his purpose." **Romans 8:28**

Your "followership" will help develop your coach's effectiveness. Of course, a person is not an effective leader unless someone is following. So, regardless of your coach's experience, you can contribute greatly to their effectiveness with your attitude as a doulos athlete. Jesus was the perfect doulos, and He still is through you.

SCAN FOR
KINGDOM SPORTS MINUTE

SCAN FOR
CHAPTER LECTURES

CHAPTER EIGHTEEN
T-E-B-S TEAM SPIRIT

No athletic team can perform at a greater capacity than the total individual abilities it contains. Yet, only when those abilities blend in just the right spirit will the team consistently maximize its performances.

ONE REMARKABLE FOOTBALL SEASON

Players on a West Coast college football team discovered the truth of that last statement as their performances were consistently great over the course of one remarkable season.

It started preseason after several starters on the offensive line had become followers of Christ. Those players began meeting together for Bible study. At one of their first meetings, as they had been discussing different passages, one of them asked, "How can we help our team be the best we can be this season?"

TWO ACTIONS

They kicked that question around a bit and decided to commit to two actions:

1. Totally go all out on every drill and assignment in each practice and game.
2. Serve and encourage teammates.

Throughout the season, each day in practice, each guy gave his own great effort. Even when exhausted, they encouraged their teammates…as well and helped bring equipment out to the field before some of the practices.

In games, they excelled in completing their assignment on each play, one play at a time. And every time a running back was tackled, one or two of the linemen would help him get to his feet.

WHAT HAPPENED

The team went undefeated, and all the main football polls voted it college football's number-one team. That 1972 USC football team is still regarded as one of the greatest college football teams of all time.

After the season, my friend who had been ministering to those offensive linemen asked one of the assistant coaches how it looked for the next season. He replied, "Next season, on paper, we will have an even better team, but we probably won't repeat as national champions."

Of course, the coach's comment surprised my friend, and he asked why.

"This season," the coach replied, "we had an offensive line that was really great. But more than what they did physically, they inspired the entire team. Because of them, we didn't have one bad practice all season. The problem is we won't have them back next season. They are all graduating."

Isn't it amazing how a team-first mentality can be contagious and help an already good team become one of the greatest of all time?

ACHIEVING THE GREATEST TEAM SPIRIT

Being a Christian athlete, you can be instrumental in developing the highest form of team spirit on your team, too. To help it become the greatest it can be.

As you focus on Jesus and yield to the Holy Spirit to express Jesus through you to your teammates and coaches, here are four ways He wants to do that. The acronym TEBS can help you get a grip on the four:

T – E – B- S

TREAT EACH PERSON AS A TEN ON A 10-POINT SCALE

In Jesus' day, Jewish people thought of tax collectors as traitors. They were Jewish men collecting money from other Jewish people for King Herod Antipas, whose allegiance was to the Romans, occupiers of their land.

To make matters worse, those tax-collecting "traitors" were also greedy. They would collect more money than the law required them to collect. If somebody refused to pay, Roman soldiers were on hand to provide the physical force to back up the tax collector's demand.

Tax collectors were social outcasts, so it must have been a shock for the people walking with Jesus that day when He stopped in front of Levi's tax booth.

Jesus raised His arm and, perhaps with an inviting motion of His hand, said, "Follow me."

What a contrast between how Jesus treated Levi—with a warm invitation to become one of His disciples—and how the rest of the people treated him—with contempt.

Jesus treated Levi as a ten on a 10-point scale when nobody else treated him as if he were even on the scale. Treating someone like a ten means looking beyond their surface.

Potential is not on the surface. In fact, many potentially great inventions were first rejected because they didn't appear to have value.

For example, when Alexander Bell tried to get financial backing for his invention, a banker told him to remove the "toy" from his office. The banker failed to see how that "toy," which was later called "telephone," would one day revolutionize communication.

Real value is not always apparent on the surface.

One way the Holy Spirit wants to express Jesus through you is by treating your teammates and coaches as a 10. In doing so, God will draw out each person's real value, which will do well for your team.

ENTER THE WORLD OF OTHERS

Jesus physically entered our world. The apostle Paul wrote that Jesus "emptied himself, taking the form of a bondservant…" (Philippians 2:7).

Marsh White, a former professional football player and counselor at Kanakuk Kamp in Missouri, allowed the Spirit of Christ to do that through him.

One of Marsh's campers, Haywood, was a spoiled young teen who came to camp against his wishes. The only reason he came was because his dad made him.

So, with a chip on his shoulder, the young camper made up his mind that he was going to be miserable. And he was.

At the end of the first week, Haywood demanded to go home. Marsh allowed him to call home. But, on the phone, his father turned him down and insisted he stay. The young camper slammed down the phone and stomped out of the office. Back at the cabin, Haywood told Marsh that he was going to leave camp anyway and not to try to stop him.

"Stop you?" Marsh responded. "I'm not going to stop you; I'm going to help you."

"What do you mean…you're going to help me?"

"I'm going with you."

"You can't go with me. You have to stay here."

"No, I don't," Marsh insisted, "my co-counselor will cover for me. Get your gear, and let's go."

As Haywood was getting his things together, Marsh slipped out of the cabin to clear what he was doing with camp leadership. When he returned, the two set out on their journey.

After a couple of miles on the hot road, the young camper got thirsty. "Marsh," he asked, "where can we get some water?"

"Water? Hmm, I know where we can get some nice cold water a couple of miles back."

For the next few miles, there was no more talk about water. However, the young camper eventually blurted out, "Marsh, I'm really hungry. Where do you think we can get some food?"

"Well, I know one place a few miles back," Marsh answered. "Back at camp, they're having roast beef and mashed potatoes tonight. You know, with that amazing gravy."

Haywood was starting to think his idea of leaving camp was not such a great one after all. Then, about 14 miles from camp, after itching from the hot sun and road grime—and going without food and water—the young camper quietly said, "I think I'd like to go back to camp."

"Are you sure?" Marsh asked. "I kind of like it out here. I'm willing to go on."

"No," Haywood insisted, "I really want to go back to camp."

"Oh, all right, if you really want to."

Turning around, the former pro football player and his young runaway hiked 14 miles back to camp. Arriving late that night, they cleaned up, ate, and went to bed. The next day, Marsh told Haywood that he would have to work his way back to having the privileges of a camper. And the young boy quickly agreed.

During the remainder of Haywood's 26-day time at camp, which included his work details, he became the most enthusiastic of all the already-enthused campers…whistling while he worked and leading a chant with other campers at the closing ceremonies, "We want one more term!"

I asked Marsh how he was sure his plan to go with Haywood would work. "He just had to come to the end of himself," Marsh told me. "I wanted to be with him when he did."

Marsh physically and mentally entered the young boy's world and helped him come to the end of himself.

Interestingly, Marsh didn't enter Haywood's world to tell Haywood what he ought to do…how he needed to shape up. He entered Haywood's world to help the young camper make his own right choices.

One way the Holy Spirit wants to express Jesus through you is by entering the world of your teammates… perhaps by discussing their dreams, relationships, likes/dislikes, and frustrations with them.

Marsh and Haywood developed a special bond because of their time together. As you enter your teammates' world, one by one, God will bond you into a team that cares about each other.

1. *How might the two actions that the USC linemen took affect your team if you and other Christians on the team should do the same?*
2. *Specifically, in what ways might Jesus treat your teammates as a ten on a 10-point scale?*
3. *Explain how Marsh going on the road with his young camper could apply to Jesus living through you with your teammates.*

T– E – **B** - S

BUILD UP OTHERS WITH POSITIVE WORDS

For two years, I was part of a team of athletes that traveled in RVs throughout the United States, putting on strength programs and sharing about Jesus with high school and college students.

Our team members had become close friends. And, like many tight groups, we enjoyed joking with each other. It was fun to kid with each other about bad habits and weaknesses.

On Thanksgiving Day, a friend of our team came over to enjoy pumpkin pie with us. He caught us at one of those moments when we were at our best in putting each other down. Our friend had been with us for about an hour when he finally said, "It almost sounds like you don't like each other."

His remark surprised us. "Of course, we like each other," we all assured him. "That's why we rip each other."

Our friend diplomatically showed us a Bible passage that caused us to look closely at what we were doing. I read it aloud for all of us.

"Let no corrupting talk come out of your mouths, but only such as is good for building up, as fits the occasion, that it may give grace to those who hear." Ephesians 4:29

At first, we tried to rationalize that those words couldn't really apply to us since we were such good friends. But, when we later discussed the passage, the Holy Spirit convinced us it did apply.

The word "corrupting," or "unwholesome," as it reads in some translations, refers to something rotten and putrid. For example, if a few dead fish were left in the hot sun for three or four days, their putrid odor could be described as corrupting or unwholesome.

Paul used the word in this passage to describe any words coming from a Christian that do not reflect Christ. We all made the connection between corrupting or unwholesome and our cutting words.

We agreed that our put-down words, although they were spoken in fun, occasionally caused hurt feelings. Our question was, what kind of words did God want us to use? That's where the word "edification" comes in.

Edification means to build up. It could be used to describe the building of a house, which, of course, can be a slow process. In building a house, we first begin with a solid foundation. Once the foundation is ready, we put the frames together. It's a process, like building up a person with sincere and positive words.

In Jesus' day, people feared leprosy. It was a grotesque-looking disease. Nodules, or lumps, would grow on a person's hands and face. The nodules would crack and leak a rotten, smelly fluid as they grew.

The leper's vocal cords would become ulcerated, which would cause his voice to be raspy. Then, the leper's eyebrows would fall out. Along with severe pain in his joints, his skin would eventually be covered with ugly, discolored patches.

A person who had this severe form of leprosy usually lived for about nine years with the disease before he lost his mind, slipped into a coma, and eventually died.

Nobody wanted to be around a leper because the disease was thought to be contagious. To set lepers apart, they were required to wear torn clothes and not be in physical contact with anybody. In fact, they could come no closer than six feet.

To make sure that people stayed away from lepers, the diseased person had to warn people of their presence by shouting, "Unclean, unclean, unclean!" That's like someone shouting, "I'm ugly, and I stink. Keep your distance." All sense of self-worth had long been shattered.

One day, as Jesus and His friends were walking through a town, a leper—without the usual warning shouts—hobbled up to Jesus and dropped to his knees in front of Him.

He looked up at Jesus through crusty eyelids and begged, "If you are willing, you can make me clean."

Even if Jesus had decided to heal the leper, He could have insisted that the leper kept the proper six-foot distance from Him. But He didn't.

Jesus reached down, putting His hand on the man's sore-infested face, and said these sincere and positive words: "Of course, I'm willing. Be cleansed."

Immediately, the leprosy vanished. The discolored patches on the man's skin cleared up. The ulcerated nodules covered much of his body, and their foul stench disappeared.

Yes, the personal touch on the leper's face was special. No way did the diseased man expect an actual touch. However, it was those words of Jesus that touched the man's soul...and caused the disease to disappear as if it had never been present.

One way the Holy Spirit wants to express Jesus through you is by speaking sincere, positive, and upbuilding words to your teammates. Words that, over time, can affect them as much as Jesus' words affected the leper's sense of self-worth.

1. *How do you think Jesus' words affected the leper?*
2. *Why must your words be both sincere and positive?*
3. *What are the different ways Jesus might want to serve your teammates through you?*
4. *Tie T-E-B-S together as Jesus' approach relates to your team.*

T – E –B - **S**

SERVING IS THE GREATEST TEAM BUILDER

The road to Jerusalem could have been a few degrees hotter than usual. At least, it might have seemed that way for 12 ego-centered men who were still smoldering from arguing about who was the greatest among them.

When those men and Jesus arrived for the Passover celebration, the city was already crowded. The Jewish people looked forward to visiting Jerusalem. Friends and relatives would enjoy catching up and eating a themed Passover meal together.

However, this Passover would be even more special for Jesus. He knew it would be the last meal He would have with His men before His crucifixion. The 13 men approached the house where a meal had already been prepared, and Jesus led them up the outdoor stairs to a guest room.

The men walked inside and saw that everything was in place. Well, almost everything. The tables were arranged in their usual horseshoe shape. The ends of several low benches, one for each man, abutted the tables. But something was missing.

Normally, before you enter a house, a low-ranking servant would be at the doorway to remove the guests' sandals and wash their feet.

Before a person went to a social gathering, they would bathe at a public bathhouse. And they would start out clean.

However, when they got to the gathering, their feet would be dirty from walking on the dusty and sometimes muddy roads. Foot washing would be refreshing for the guests.

The servant would be at the doorway to remove the sandals from each guest and wash his feet. After the foot washing, the guest would join the other guests and recline on a bench at the banquet table.

However, when Jesus and His men entered this upper room, no servant was on hand to wash their feet. Maybe the servant was sick or not reliable. Or, quite likely, Jesus Himself might have dismissed the servant just to see how His disciples would handle the situation.

It was a common practice that whenever a servant was not on hand, one of the guests would volunteer to wash everyone's feet. But it would be a scorching day at the North Pole before any of Jesus' proud disciples would get down on his knees and scrub between the toes of the other men.

Everyone had been at the table for a while when Jesus decided it was time for action. As He pushed Himself up from his low bench, the other men most likely stopped eating and followed Him closely with their eyes.

Why didn't I do this? each man must have thought. Pride, men. That's why you didn't assume the role of a low-ranking servant. Now, your leader is going to do what you should have done.

Jesus pulled up His outer robe and slipped it over His head. Then He picked up one of the towels—the "uniform" for a common slave—and wrapped it around His waist.

After pouring water from the pitcher into a basin, He carried the basin over to the feet of one of His men. Jesus knelt on the floor, removed the man's sandals, and washed his feet.

One of the USC linemen's actions was finding ways to serve their teammates. Sometimes, it was just to give a listening and non-judgmental ear. Other times, it was in providing a ride, buying a meal, or...any number of things.

One way the Holy Spirit wants to express Jesus through you is by serving your teammates and coaches. As He does, your team will be closer to performing at its maximum.

In union with Jesus, applying His TEBS approach to your team might not develop your team into one of the greatest of all time. But you will experience God developing your team into being the greatest that the total of all its abilities will allow it to be.

SCAN FOR
KINGDOM SPORTS MINUTE

SCAN FOR
CHAPTER LECTURES

Made in the USA
Monee, IL
09 September 2025

24294418R00085